PSYCHEDELIC CELLULOID

Oldcastle Books

SIMON MATTHEWS

PSYCHEDELIC CELLULOID

British Pop Music in Film and TV 1965-1974

Oldcastle Books

First published in 2016 by
Oldcastle Books Ltd,
PO Box 394, Harpenden,
AL5 1XJ, UK
oldcastlebooks.co.uk
@PsychedelicOal

ISBN
978-1-84344-457-2 (Print)
978-1-84344-458-9 (Epub)
978-1-84344-459-6 (Kindle)
978-1-84344-460-2 (Pdf)

2 4 6 8 10 9 7 5 3 1

Typeset and designed by Elsa Mathern
Printed in China

For
Candy and a Currant Bun

CONTENTS

INTRODUCTION

In his seminal study of the genesis, birth and flowering of UK pop culture, George Melly called it a 'revolt into style': the moment the UK collectively burst out of the monochrome cocoon of the 50s and into the dazzling colours, designs and optimism of the 60s. The rapidity of the change is something which – in itself – confirmed to Melly and other observers that, due to its transience, this was a truly 'pop' event. The enormous difference in style and approach between the two eras, concertinaed into just a few years, is best illustrated by watching two films directed by Michael Winner: *West 11* and *The Jokers*.

The former, made in black and white and set in a dingy room in the then slum district of Notting Hill Gate (thus making it a companion piece to The *L-Shaped Room*), is resolutely 'kitchen sink', perhaps hardly surprising given that its script came from the pen of Keith Waterhouse, whose other cinema credits at this point included *Whistle Down the Wind*, *A Kind of Loving* and *Billy Liar*. *West 11* is bleak. Dismal street scenes where gangs of children kick balls along canyons of ill-kept tall Victorian houses, pockmarked by bomb sites, unworried by traffic; the cast and extras wear nondescript clothes with no immediate or discernible style and eat hurried little meals in basic street corner cafes. The central character, played by Alfred Lynch, who after this rare leading role was seen mainly on TV, seeks solace in popping pills, rejects Roman Catholicism (shades here of Graham Greene) and hangs out at the local jazz club; a cramped basement, this features apparently unamplified performances from Ken Colyer's Jazzmen and the Tony Kinsey Quartet. The former, respected and fiercely inscrutable pioneers of the UK 'trad' scene, the latter an offshoot of the Johnny Dankworth Seven, playing cool hard bop with a UK rather than a US tinge. The audience dances politely, jives (slightly), drinks coffee and orange juice or sits out numbers on the floors leaning back against the cellar wall such is the lack of furniture. Diana Dors cruises around, hoping to pick up a man, much as she did in *Dance Hall* (50). *West 11*, which came with a marvellously evocative title theme from Acker Bilk - quite the

A key early success for Michael Winner

best thing he recorded and now very hard to come by - was filmed in the spring of 63, some six months after *That Was the Week That Was* had begun knocking holes in the reputation of Harold Macmillan and was released at the point the Profumo scandal ushered in the brief era of Sir Alec Douglas-Home. Although The Beatles had already secured their first US number one with 'She Loves You', at the point *West 11* appeared it still looks like the England of rationing, shortages and national service.

Just three years later, Winner was directing *The Jokers*... resolutely undingy... and featuring Oliver Reed (ascending to stardom via this film) and Michael Crawford, midway between his roles in *The Knack* and *How I Won the War*, skidding around the posh bits of London in a Mini Moke and narrowly avoiding the band of the Grenadier Guards *en route* to the Trooping of the Colour. Reed and Crawford spend much of their time at night clubs or society parties (during which the film includes split second appearances from two as yet unidentified pop groups of the era) before they career off to the strains of the Peter and Gordon title theme to rob the Tower of London. The film is in colour. The cast is mainly young. They wear the latest clothes. The interiors look like the 60s rather than the 20s. The script jettisons the social realism of *West 11* and is amiable, contemporary, flip and paced like a situation comedy. *The Jokers* is clearly a pop film of the sort that would have been unthinkable a few years earlier... when pop music itself, before the sudden appearance of the pirate radio stations in 64, was confined in the UK to a mere five hours air time per week.

In his narrative, Melly, perhaps hardly surprisingly given his own Liverpudlian origins, identifies The Beatles as the key drivers of this change and punctuates his account with regular bulletins about their progress through the decade. The case for British pop cinema beginning – and ending – with The Beatles is indeed strong. Although there had been earlier pop films, and both Tommy Steele and Cliff Richard had reached film star status (in the UK domestic market, if nowhere else), neither the films nor their major players had a significant global impact, nor did their style permeate society as a whole. The huge success of *A Hard Day's Night* – the ninth biggest grossing film in America in 64 – was the single event that brought serious US studio money to London and kickstarted the whole genre. Shot in early 64 and released in July that year, *A Hard Day's Night* may have cemented The Beatles' success

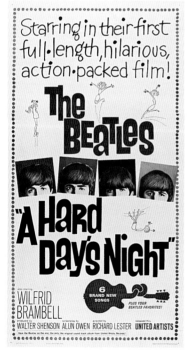

The best selling pop film of 1964 – and did better business in the US than Elvis Presley's Viva Las Vegas

and brought dollars flooding into the UK. But is it a typical Swinging London film? Despite boasting sequences shot in John Aspinall's W1 casino Les Ambassadeurs (one of the rarefied trend-setting pinnacles around which much of what followed would revolve), it much more closely resembles the preceding genre of 'kitchen sink' dramas. The characters emerge from the North of England. It is shot in black and white. The script is by Alun Owen, whose previous credits included many working class social realist TV dramas and the screenplay for the crime thriller *The Criminal*; the supporting cast includes Norman Rossington, previously seen in *Saturday Night and Sunday Morning* and the incomparable Wilfred Brambell, moonlighting here from his grotesque duties in *Steptoe and Son*. Its key difference was that it dropped the usual downbeat, grimy, approach of its predecessors and offered its audience instead an optimistic, zestful and youth-orientated narrative. These ingredients owed much to its director, Richard Lester, an astute choice for the gig. A child prodigy from Philadelphia, resident in the UK since the early 50s, Lester first came to attention directing the 61 pop film *It's Trad Dad*, which, despite a hackneyed putting-on-a-show plot, was interspersed with superbly designed and shot musical interludes that predated music videos by two decades. He followed this with the Cold War/space race satire *The Mouse on The Moon*, which surprised many by being a modest success on the US college and campus circuit. Importantly, Lester had Goon connections too. With Lennon, in particular, holding the madcap surrealism of Milligan and Sellers in high regard, Lester's work on the TV series *A Show Called Fred* in the mid 50s and his award winning short *The Running Jumping and Standing Still Film* (59) commended him further. Stylistically *A Hard Day's Night* and the productions that flooded on to the cinema screens of Britain from 65 onwards also owed much to selected European cinema releases of just a few years earlier: the high fashion and seemingly improvised plot of *La Dolce Vita*, the freewheeling youthfulness of *Jules et Jim*, the classic young-people-in-a city storyline of *Bonjour Tristesse* and the elegant combination of sexuality and music in *Una Ragazza Nuda/Strip-Tease* (starring Nico with songs by Serge Gainsbourg). All are quite unlike the diet of war films, Rattiganesque drawing-room dramas and eccentric comedies that prevailed in the UK for many years after 45. The case for Richard Lester being the key *auteur* of the UK pop film of the 60s and 70s is strong indeed and it is ironic that the discarding of this baggage, and its replacement by films in which music, graphic design and inventive title

Scene through the eye of a lens: Richard Lester, auteur of the Swinging London genre

sequences predominated, owed a great deal to two external influences – a US director (Lester – whose first major success brought in US money) and European art house cinema.

Flushed with the success of *A Hard Day's Night* Lester moved quickly on to his next two projects. These appeared within a few weeks of each other in 65 and really did establish the UK pop film genre: an adaptation of the Ann Jellicoe play *The Knack* and *Help!*, a sequel for The Beatles. The former was an immaculate blend of dialogue, visual imagery, music and fashion that was so striking in its tone that at least one critic described himself as leaving the cinema in a state of euphoria after seeing it. The latter placed The Beatles at the centre of an absurd chase/caper plot – which would have suited Buster Keaton fifty years earlier – and had them performing a dozen songs in various costumes and locations. Slightly less successful than *A Hard Day's Night*, it nevertheless inspired many imitations as well as the massively popular TV series starring The Monkees. It was, predictably, an enormous US success.

The big Hollywood studios now unveiled popular entertainments like *Alfie*, *Georgy Girl* and *Modesty Blaise* as well as *Blow-Up*, MGM's venture into the serious ultra-stylish European art house market. During the course of 66, all of these outstripped *Help!* at the box office, whilst in 67 *To Sir, With Love* did better business than all of them, and remains the biggest grossing example of the type even today. The latish spin-off from the early 60s satire boom, *Bedazzled*, from 20th Century Fox, did well too. Such was the appetite for anything English that big US studios were happy to distribute virtually any film with a pop – or youth – angle, thus ensuring that finance could be raised for productions like *The Jokers*, *How I Won the War* (Lester again), *Smashing Time*, *Up the Junction* and *Only When I Larf*. Nor was the boom restricted to major UK and US film producers. Would-be independent *auteurs* flocked to London from many parts of the world, hoping for a slice of the action, discovering in the process that London was easy to film in, there were few permits or taxes that needed to be paid and professional domestic film crews were easily available. Both *The Mini-Affair* and *Popdown* were made by US independent film makers hoping to make a killing, whilst the mega-success of *Blow-Up* resulted, in time, in several European directors shooting in London and carefully incorporating – somewhere in their plot – the latest group or singer in either acting or musical roles. The launch in late 67, by The Beatles, of their Apple boutique in Baker Street W1 (which duly appears in the film *Hot Millions*) seems emblematic of this first flourish of activity: a major happening combining music, fashion and design. But, again, it's worth remembering that the striking mural on the side of the building (setting it aside from its rather dowdy neighbours) was designed by the Dutch design collective The Fool, which a year later would bring out their own folkrock LP, another rather ironic instance of how much of Swinging London came from abroad. Opening a hip clothes shop was not, as it transpired, the limit of The Beatles' ambitions. In the summer of 67 they established Apple Films, to produce their BBC TV Special *Magical Mystery Tour*. The intention was that this would be the first of a series of pioneering and artistically adventurous credits from a new youth-orientated UK studio. The feature length cartoon *Yellow Submarine* and the psychedelic mood piece *Wonderwall* duly appeared as the earliest, and possibly the best, examples of its work.

The Apple boutique during its brief flowering on an otherwise dowdy London street corner

The US-funded boom in British films continued through 68 and 69 – despite Swinging London then beginning to recede somewhat – with productions such as *Mrs Brown, You've Got a Lovely Daughter*, *Otley*, *The Bliss of Mrs Blossom*, *The Guru* and *If It's Tuesday, This Must Be Belgium*, the latter a major box office success. It even extended, remarkably perhaps, into explicitly UK dramas such as *The Virgin Soldiers* and *The Reckoning*. Some commentators wondered at the continued US preference for anything London – but films often take a long time to shoot, edit, dub and complete and money committed in 66-67 was still trickling through the system some years later. European finance was also significant during this period, whether being spent in London itself (*Nerosubianco* and *Sympathy for the Devil*) or elsewhere (*The Girl on a Motorcycle*). The phenomenon peaked in 69-70 when, bolstered by the apparent certainty of lucrative US distribution deals, UK filmmakers produced a crop of inventive releases including *The Magic Christian*, *Take a Girl Like You*, *The Breaking of Bumbo* (all adapted from novels), *Loot*, *Connecting Rooms* and *Entertaining Mr Sloane* (all plays) and completely original projects such as *Joanna*, *The Touchables*, *Leo the Last* and *Performance*. Most of these boasted a resident group or a singer in an acting role and had a strong eye on the burgeoning soundtrack LP market. A plethora of European art house releases also appeared at the same time, mining much the same seam – *More*, *Paroxismus*, *Deep End*, *Cannabis* and *Alba pagana*. Indeed, by the end of the decade, the pop film style had seeped everywhere: into horror with *The Haunted House of Horror*, into sci-fi with *Moon Zero Two* and into comedy via *What's Good for the Goose*. The last, an attempt to ingratiate himself with the youth market by veteran comedian Norman Wisdom, was not dissimilar to a number of dramas that appeared in the aftermath of the September 68 relaxation of censorship in the UK. Most had plots centred on the age of consent (*All the Right Noises*, *Twinky*) and generally featured middle aged men enjoying relationships with sexually available younger girls. It was a trend that, whatever its reasonably stylish and legitimate origins, spiralled down quickly into the tackiness of the 70s UK sex film.

Picking a moment when the canon peaked, one would surely settle on 70. By that point, two additional sub-genres had appeared, expanding the broader parameters of the pop film and reflecting the increased independence and spending power of youth compared to previous generations. The first of these was the concert movie, usually a sprawling semi-improvised documentary about a particular event (*Supershow*, *Amougies*, *Love and Music* and *Glastonbury Fayre*). Ironically, this had been pioneered in the UK with *Charlie is my Darling*, the 66 Rolling Stones film that never made it into the cinemas and later, on a modest scale, by DA Pennebaker's *Don't Look Back*; but only really took off after the massive US success of *Monterey Pop* (also Pennebaker) in the summer of 68. The second was the emergence of the serious experimental art film, decked out with progressive music, shown at film societies and in student unions on the ever expanding network of universities and polytechnics, at late night showings in Odeons, Gaumonts and ABCs and in the nascent independent cinemas: *The Body* and *Continental Circus* come to mind, as do early works by Werner Herzog and Rainer Werner Fassbinder.

DA Pennebaker zooms in on Dylan during his 1965 UK tour

1970 also saw the filming of *A Clockwork Orange*, which yielded the biggest selling pop soundtrack LP of the era and *Get Carter*. Both were astonishingly successful at the box office, only to be dogged by misfortune. The former was pulled from the distribution circuit after public demonstrations against its extreme sex and violence, whilst the latter, despite topping the US viewing charts for three weeks between *Love Story* and *Summer of '42* – remarkable for such an impenetrably British film – quickly disappeared from sight. There would be no sequels, and *Get Carter* did not inaugurate a UK equivalent of the French genre of realistic and creative crime dramas. In reality, something so dependent on US money and distribution deals couldn't last and, once all the major US studios posted losses at the end of the 60s, the funding of ventures in London quickly dried up. Apart from purely internal Hollywood problems it can hardly have helped – in the perception that studio bosses had about the marketability of pop films – that The Beatles broke up in 70 (as did Herman's Hermits and The Dave Clark Five, the two other most significant UK pop groups in terms of sales in the US in the mid and late 60s) and The Rolling Stones moved into tax exile not long after. The suddenness of the change is best illustrated by Terence Stamp who, when interviewed in 2013 (doing publicity for his role in *Song for Marion*), drily commented '... when the 60s ended, so did I...' If one of the greatest faces of the era, internationally acclaimed after roles in *Modesty Blaise*, *Far from the Madding Crowd* and *Poor Cow* and a string of elegant European ventures such as *Blue, Theorem* and *The Mind of Mr Soames*, couldn't command a single decent leading role, what hope was there for other stars created in such a fragile boom? With the exception of Michael Caine and Oliver Reed, very little it would seem. Rita Tushingham experienced a major career gap after 69, David Warner did little post 70, David Hemmings left for an abortive trip to Hollywood in 71 and Hywel Bennett spent more time in TV than film from 72. All had been major box office draws just a few years earlier and all had disappeared from sight by 73.

By the mid 70s, the UK film industry was in low gear. Although EMI remained active, there was less money around, less willingness to invest (even modestly) in original ideas or experimentation and a tendency, instead, to rely on reliable formulas, preferably with a nostalgic bent. For every *Wicker Man* or *Zardoz* there were innumerable TV adaptations. Hemdale, the major UK hope of only a few years earlier, faded away after producing *Connecting Rooms*, *Melody* and *Boy Stroke Girl*, none of which was a hit, and distributing the mega-flop *Universal Soldier*. The continuing reduction in cinemas and rise in TV ownership were also factors. Although the overall numbers of productions did not decline catastrophically, the figures tended to be bulked out by US (or foreign) films shot in UK studios. In terms of purely domestic product it would be fair to say that, by 73-74, it consisted of an annual *Bond*, a *Carry On* and a couple of *Hammers*, all graced by increasingly elderly casts, TV spin-offs, annual additions to the *Adventures of* and

Confessions of sex comedy series, and below that, a slew of adult only sex films – most now long forgotten – of almost no merit. Pop groups and pop singers in acting roles tended not to be seen at all. In the end, Apple, even Apple, underpinned by the riches of The Beatles, ended film production in 74 after releasing its last two productions *Son of Dracula* and *Little Malcolm and His Struggle Against the Eunuchs*, both of which had started shooting a couple of years earlier. They made almost zero impact when released and this effectively brought the era of the UK pop film to a close... a rather sad fizzling out of what had briefly seemed an era of limitless possibilities.

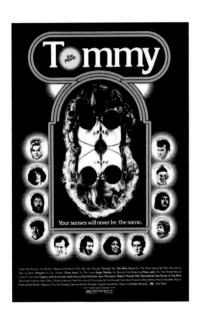

A few films with pop music did continue to appear, of course, but they were no longer representative of UK productions as a whole. *Tommy* (75), Ken Russell's multi-star extravaganza, did well in the US and duly spawned *Quadrophenia*, which was filmed in 78 and premiered at Cannes in 79. The problem was: *Tommy*, with its enormous cast and big production values, was rather like a rock musical version of *It's a Mad, Mad, Mad World* or *Those Magnificent Men in their Flying Machines*, whilst *Quadrophenia*, when it appeared, was already anachronistic in much the same way *That'll Be the Day* and *Stardust* had been a few years earlier. The relative success (but only in the UK) of *Quadrophenia* was followed by *Breaking Glass* with its traditional glum rags to riches/road to ruin plot and *The Great Rock 'n' Roll Swindle*, a deliberate, and entertaining, pastiche (by Malcolm McLaren) of much earlier productions like *The Tommy Steele Story* and *Expresso Bongo* in a provocative style that owed more than a little to Serge Gainsbourg. Unlike Gainsbourg, though, McLaren did not go on to have a major career in film.

Thereafter, things were bleak indeed. Although George Harrison returned – with Handmade Films – to produce *Life of Brian* in 78-79 after EMI had pulled out, and followed this with *The Long Good Friday* and *Time Bandits*, anything to do with the contemporary British pop scene was conspicuous by its absence on screen. The major groups and singers of the 80s and 90s were not automatically drafted in to spy thrillers, offered major acting roles or casually seen in obligatory discotheque scenes. Nor were they the immediate choice for composing or performing film themes. Homage to the genre was a long time arriving, and when it finally did, came – as so much had between 65 and 74 – from the US. *Austin Powers : International*

Man of Mystery (97) appeared shortly after the first flowering of 'Brit Pop', whose major exponents Blur, The Verve, Suede, Oasis, Pulp and Elastica pillaged heavily from the musical legacy of the 60s and 70s with many – dozens, actually – of referential borrowings from and tributes to the UK pop films of the period. It is interesting, perhaps, to speculate that *Austin Powers*, which began shooting in 96, was seen as a commercially attractive project in Hollywood after the success in the US of Suede and Oasis. It starred a gormless central figure (apparently channelling the late Simon Dee) rigged out à la George Lazenby in his sole Bond outing in 69 in a blue velvet suit and ruffed shirt, who duly crashes through a variety of ludicrous encounters as a secret agent. Michael York co-starred – selected partly on the basis of his (much) earlier roles in films like *Smashing Time* and *The Guru* – and it even came with a contribution on its soundtrack by The Mike Flowers Pops (whose major hit during this period was an immaculately tongue-in-cheek lounge version of the Oasis song '*Wonderwall*', whose title, of course, was culled from the 68 film), parodying the easy listening themes of Burt Bacharach. *Austin Powers* was sufficiently successful to spawn two sequels, which were enormous box office hits in 99 and 02 respectively. Thereafter, British cinema also caught up with its predecessors, producing a number of elegant and well made dramas of which *Lock, Stock and Two Smoking Barrels* (98) and *Layer Cake* (04) were the most notable. The former borrowed heavily from the semi-comic crime capers of the 60s whilst the latter owed much to gritty realistic films like *Get Carter*. Like *Austin Powers*, both were noted for their soundtrack LPs, substantial artefacts in their own right, which mixed a wide variety of material culled from the present and past; something the films of the 60s and 70s would not have done, concentrating as they mainly did on completely contemporary music.

The narrative here could continue … but now is the time to look, one by one, at what makes up the mother lode. Selecting the films required defining – somehow – what should and should not be considered a UK Pop film. It seemed common sense that the definition should embrace any film featuring a UK pop singer (or group) of the period in acting roles, or appearing in a specific scene or credited on the soundtrack, usually, if in the latter capacity, performing the title song or theme. Beyond that, anything with a specifically 'youth' angle in terms of cast, plot, design or appeal seemed appropriate. Inevitably, though, even these parameters produced anomalies. What about the *Bond*

The ultimate homage to the world of late '60's early '70's UK feature films, albeit played as parody, and created by Mike Myers – a Canadian long resident in London

films? Although raided extensively for the *Austin Powers* franchise, and with some iconic music, Bond himself was hardly a child of the 60s: a fortyish leading man, who'd served in the war, he was clearly designed to appeal to adults. Putting 007 to one side, therefore, and starting with *The Knack* and *Help!* made sense, and treating *A Hard Day's Night*, *Darling* and *Morgan – A Suitable Case for Treatment* as late examples of the preceding period justified. Over three hundred productions emerged, some from the fog of history, some hardly seen since their release (if indeed they were ever released), and are collected here in chronological order, irrespective of whether they are film or TV productions or whether they are UK or European in origin. As this book covers British pop, purely US films are generally excluded, though a few that featured British singers and bands did creep in to the listings. The appendices provide listings of features of lesser significance, shorts, documentaries and TV dramas... anything, in fact, that might seem relevant to the topic. Excluded are *Top of the Pops, Ready, Steady Go!* and many other UK TV series that ran for years on end and specifically featured the latest pop acts: compiling a listing of these was impossible (many episodes now being wiped) and this book is not an attempt to catalogue them. Travelling through the period and assembling images and an accompanying text yielded some strange facts. Who could identify which UK group appeared in, or contributed to, the highest number of film and TV ventures during this period? Neither The Beatles nor The Rolling Stones gained this accolade. The most prominent performers in front of the cameras between 65 and 74 turned out to be Pink Floyd, who worked on eight features and two shorts, appeared in a major Belgian TV special, can be heard on the soundtrack of two other features and might have had something to do with the Spanish film *Salome* (if anyone ever finds a copy and manages to investigate). They even had time to turn down *A Clockwork Orange*. Critics may yet speculate how much their musical development away from quirky psych-pop to the long tonal pieces that eventually made them the biggest band in the world in the mid 70s might have been down to the influence of composing music for films...

Now read on!

Set the Controls
for the Heart of W1!

Not everyone would turn down the chance to work with Stanley Kubrick but the inability of Pink Floyd to agree terms about the use of *'Atom Heart Mother'* in *A Clockwork Orange* – although a *faux pas* in subsequently denying them royalties from an astonishingly successful soundtrack LP – simply wasn't that critical, for them, in terms of their career development.

Dubbed 'the light kings of England' by their US label Tower, their screen credits between 66 and 72 were prodigious: the Peter Whitehead short *London 66-67*, later expanded into the documentary feature *Tonite Let's All Make Love in London*, a promo-film for their debut single *'Arnold Layne'*, live concert footage in *Dope* (co-produced by DA Pennebaker, but rarely if ever seen), a slot in the Belgian pop TV film *Vibrato*, an album's worth of unreleased music for *The Committee*, live footage in the US documentary short *San Francisco*, an extract of *'Interstellar Overdrive'* used in *The Touchables*, the soundtrack for *More*, another soundtrack, mostly unreleased, for *Zabriskie Point*, background music for the documentary feature *The Body*, appearances in two of the post-*Monterey Pop* concert films of the period, *Amougies* and *Stamping Ground* and the soundtrack for *La Vallée*. Other curiosities include the Spanish feature *Salome* (70) which claims to include on its

soundtrack a rearrangement, by Jorge Pi (of the Bilbao Blues Band), of the Pink Floyd arrangement of *'Salome'* by Richard Strauss and the use of their material in two Kung Fu films: *Fist of Fury* (71) and *Intimate Confessions of a Chinese Courtesan* (72).

Given that the group started out sharing a house with Mike Leonard, an architect who devised and built optical effects for use on stage and film, went on to use specially commissioned light shows by Peter Wynne-Willson and whose original lead guitarist Syd Barrett lived with pop artist Duggie Fields, with hindsight it's hardly surprising that they spent almost as much of their time composing film music or appearing in front of the cameras as they did on tour and recording.

THE KNACK

Richard Lester directs
Michael Crawford and Rita Tushingham star

A Richard Lester adaptation of an Ann Jellicoe play, originally performed at the Royal Court Theatre in 1962, *The Knack* stars Rita Tushingham – an absolutely iconic female star of the period after roles in *A Taste of Honey*, *Girl with the Green Eyes* and *The Leather Boys* – as a young, single woman arriving by train in London who ends up sharing a house with Ray Brooks (an immaculately dressed, very hip and predatory musician), Michael Crawford (a sex-starved teacher) and Donal Donnelly (an eccentric artist).

Beautifully made and the epitome of cool, Swinging London, the film projects an optimistic feeling that almost anything might be possible and is brilliantly shot in the style of Lester's previous mega-success *A Hard Day's Night*. Unlike preceding dramas in which anyone under 30 was, at best, just a supporting figure in a larger cast, *The Knack* – in which Crawford and Tushingham explore newly available sexual freedoms and clumsily try to get 'the knack' of successfully establishing relationships with the opposite sex – is almost entirely orientated towards young people. *The Knack* thus makes a good claim to be considered the first feature film to adopt this typically 60's youth centric approach to its storyline whilst still being firmly targeted at the wider adult audience. Hugely liked at the time, it won the Palme d'Or at Cannes.

The very jazzy soundtrack was by John Barry, with contributions from Alan Haven and Johnny de Little (formerly vocalist in The John Barry Seven). Haven was an ideal choice – a jazz organist married to the then Miss World who had simultaneously composed and released '*Image*' the popular instrumental used as a theme by Radio Caroline.

Released 3 June 1965, 85 minutes, black and white
DVD: released by Twentieth Century Fox, August 2004
SOUNDTRACK: released on United Artists in 1965.
Reissued on Simply Vinyl in 2001

Rita Tushingham reads about Paul Klee

HELP!

Richard Lester directs
The Beatles star

The Beatles on Salisbury Plain

For the second Beatles picture Richard Lester was given a significantly bigger budget than that available for *A Hard Day's Night*. This allowed him to film in colour and to base some parts of the plot abroad: the sections in *Help!* set in a ski resort and the Bahamas duly followed. Shot by Lester almost simultaneously with his work on *The Knack*, the script was written by US novelist Marc Behm (whose previous credit was the Cary Grant-Audrey Hepburn thriller *Charade*) and UK playwright Charles Wood. This replaces the semi-documentary approach of *A Hard Day's Night* with a surreal comedy-caper about an Indian cult chasing Ringo (not dissimilar in style to Lester's previous credit *Mouse on The Moon*) interspersed with carefully set and choreographed songs, each resembling a music video – a format Lester had earlier used in *It's Trad Dad* (1961). Leo McKern, Eleanor Bron and Victor Spinetti co-star, the last something of a fixture in The Beatles *entourage* at this point.

An immense success at the box office, the film was noted for the high levels of cannabis consumed by The Beatles during its production. The end result resembles (and is arguably no better than) any single episode of the 50's BBC radio series *The Goons* (with whom, of course, both George Martin and Richard Lester had worked) expanded here with the newly available funds to an indulgent length. The sequences, often loosely related to the storyline, of The Beatles performing in various costumes and settings quickly became the *de rigueur* template for most pop group films, being copied with great success by The Monkees *et al.*

The accompanying LP – which doubled as a soundtrack in the UK – was released in August 65 and reached no. 1 in virtually every territory.

Released 29 July 1965, 92 minutes, colour
DVD: released by Parlophone Records, November 2007
SOUNDTRACK: UK LP released 6 August 1965 contains solely material performed by The Beatles. US release (13 August 1965) includes tracks from George Martin and Ken Thorne and is billed as *'Original Motion Picture Soundtrack'*

After Oklahoma...

From its appearance in the early '50's, the LP was closely associated with original soundtrack or original cast recordings of film and stage musicals: *Oklahoma*, *South Pacific*, *The King and I*, *Gigi* and *West Side Story* were the mega successes of their time with chart runs of up to 20 years, easily eclipsing anything produced by other genres. The desire by the wider public for a vinyl artefact with sing-along show tunes and brooding theme music continued after the emergence of The Beatles: *Mary Poppins*, *My Fair Lady*, *The Sound of Music*, *Dr Zhivago*, *Oliver* and *Paint Your Wagon* all sold in numbers most groups and singers could have only dreamt about. Only Kubrick's *2001: A Space Odyssey* came close to matching this.

The May 67 success of *Blow-Up*, with its brief placement in the lower regions of the US Top 200, was remarkable therefore – the more so because it was written and performed by Herbie Hancock, keyboards player in the Miles Davis Quintet, supported by several fellow jazzers. UK group The Yardbirds appeared on one track. A few months later *To Sir, With Love* became the first pop film to produce a major US chart LP, starting something of a minor trend there in 68-69 when *Wild in the Streets* (Max Frost and The Troopers), *Candy* (The Byrds, Steppenwolf) and *Easy Rider* (The Byrds, Steppenwolf, Jimi Hendrix) all sold well as a younger audience emulated their parents and bought mementos of a great night out at the cinema. In the UK The Pink Floyd were the only group to create complete soundtracks and enjoy significant commercial success with *More* and *Obscured by Clouds*; whilst the sprawling triple LP released to accompany the US concert movie *Woodstock* also sold well, as did the compilation double LP issued for *That'll Be the Day*. By far the greatest success, though, for a pop or counter-culture film soundtrack during this period was *A Clockwork Orange* with its mixture of original classical, classical rescored for synthesizer and psychedelic folk.

During its peak the British pop film may have only produced a half dozen or so commercial soundtrack successes, but dozens of superb songs and hundreds of pieces of brilliant music were littered across the genre, to be disinterred, re-issued and sampled by the musical archaeologists in the decades that followed.

ALFIE

Lewis Gilbert directs
Michael Caine stars

Independently produced and directed by Lewis Gilbert, whose best known previous credits included some of the most iconic UK war films of the 50s and early 60s, from a not particularly well known 63 Bill Naughton play, *Alfie* was not initially seen as obvious box office and had a troubled genesis. Prior to being accepted by Michael Caine, the lead role was turned down by Laurence Harvey, Anthony Newley and Terence Stamp, the budget was not overly generous and Shelley Winters had to be added as a co-star to ensure a US release. Strong supporting parts were played by Millicent Martin and Julia Foster. Martin had been a mainstay

IS EVERY MAN AN ALFIE? ASK ANY GIRL!

MICHAEL CAINE IS

PARAMOUNT PICTURES presents

ALFIE

MILLICENT MARTIN • JULIA FOSTER • JANE ASHER • SHIRLEY ANNE FIELD
VIVIEN MERCHANT • ELEANOR BRON WITH SHELLEY WINTERS AS RUBY
SCREENPLAY BY BILL NAUGHTON BASED ON THE PLAY "ALFIE" BY BILL NAUGHTON • MUSIC BY SONNY ROLLINS • PRODUCED AND DIRECTED BY LEWIS GILBERT
TECHNICOLOR® TECHNISCOPE®   A LEWIS GILBERT PRODUCTION

of the TV satire show *That Was the Week That Was* whilst Foster had accrued an impressive set of credits. co-starring with Michael Crawford in *Two Left Feet* (where with hindsight his character of the hapless virginal young man was very much his dummy run for *The Knack*), with Anthony Newley in the Soho based drama *The Small World of Sammy Lee*, fitting in an acclaimed slot in NF Simpson's absurdist hit play *One Way Pendulum* and with Oliver Reed in Michael Winner's *The System*. Also featured was Jane Asher, a child star in the 50s who was, by this point, dating Paul McCartney.

The plot concerns the sexual adventures of an amoral young(ish) cockney Lothario (Caine) who – eventually – gets his comeuppance. Filmed almost entirely in and around London, it cost only $500,000 (£170,000) to make and was staggeringly successful, becoming the then biggest UK film ever in the US, and receiving 5 Academy Award nominations. Over the next few years, this duly resulted in many US studio-financed features being filmed in London whose storylines shared broadly similar parameters (tourist views of the capital + young cast + music + Swinging plot) in the anticipation that they would produce similar commercial returns. The central character proved to be so popular (the eternal single bloke, playing the field and getting into continual sexual escapades) that the film eventually produced *Alfie Darling*, a 76 sequel starring pop singer Alan Price.

The soundtrack was by jazz saxophonist Sonny Rollins and contained a Bacharach-David theme song that swiftly became one of the most widely heard and covered songs of the era. The UK recording, by Cilla Black, reached number nine when released in March 66 and was followed by US versions by Cher (number thirty two, August 66) and Dionne Warwick (number fifteen, May 67).

Released 29 March 1966, 114 minutes, colour
DVD: released by Paramount Home Entertainment, August 2002
SOUNDTRACK: LP released in UK on Impulse in 1966. Re-issued on CD in 1997

MODESTY BLAISE

Joseph Losey directs
Monica Vitti and Terence Stamp star

Made by Twentieth Century Fox and based
on a phenomenally popular strip cartoon
series in the London *Evening Standard*, the film
version of *Modesty Blaise* was one of many attempts
by a major studio to emulate the burgeoning success of
the James Bond series. Unlike Fleming's stories, though, which are
mainly concerned with the escapades of a secret agent, Modesty Blaise,
with its use of extravagant sets – some of which look as if they could have
been created by contemporary Op Artist Bridget Riley – and jet-setting
locations (London, Amsterdam, the Mediterranean), can be seen instead
as an early example of the self-consciously modern 'pop' films of the 60s.

Monica Vitti as Modesty Blaise

Directed by Joseph Losey, with a script from his long standing collaborator
Evan Jones, both of whom had previously worked on *King & Country*,
Modesty Blaise features Dirk Bogarde as an extremely effete and
enjoyable villain and stars Monica Vitti in the title role. Terence Stamp –
one of the major 'faces' of the period – co-stars as her cockney geezer
accomplice. With a flimsy plot about an attempt to steal a shipment of
diamonds, daft deadpan dialogue, gay iconography and appearances by
distinguished British gents rigged out in suits, bowler hats and umbrellas,
Modesty Blaise looks, with hindsight, not unlike a possible prototype for
the later less pop-oriented *The Italian Job*.

The film was not particularly well regarded at the time but stands up
well today. The soundtrack, by Johnny Dankworth, includes David and
Jonathan singing 'Modesty' during the opening credits.

Released May 1966, 119 minutes, colour
DVD: released 16 July 2002
SOUNDTRACK: released on Twentieth Century Records 1966.
Reissued on vinyl and CD by Harkit Records 2010

THE GAME IS OVER (LA CURÉE)

Roger Vadim directs
Jane Fonda stars

A straightforward French film of its time, *The Game is Over* enjoyed a UK and US release and, as a result, reached a wider market than usual. Filmed in France, it was directed by Roger Vadim who had previously made stars of both Brigitte Bardot and Gillian Hills and who now sought to repeat this success with his wife, Jane Fonda. Co-starring Peter McEnery, previously seen to advantage in *Victim*, and Michel Piccoli (one of seven films shot by this star in 66) the plot concerns a young wife who embarks on an affair with her stepson and the various unfortunate consequences that subsequently occur. A reasonable example of Vadim's work, it was described by one critic as '25% titillation and 75% marzipan'.

As in *La Collectionneuse*, which had The Ingoes, later Blossom Toes, the soundtrack features a UK group that would go on to greater things, in this case The Arthur Brown Set, a popular club act in Paris (where they had a residency in a strip club frequented by transvestites), prior to their rebirth as The Crazy World of Arthur Brown. The young stars and risqué and permissive plot illustrate the not inconsiderable influence that European cinema had on setting the Swinging London template.

Vadim's next project, *Barbarella*, was a French-Italian production aimed squarely at the US market. Filmed in late 67 to early 68, and based on a popular French comic strip adapted by Terry Southern, it paired Fonda with John Phillip Law (another US expatriate in Europe, and previously in the spaghetti western *Death Rides a Horse*), Anita Pallenberg and David Hemmings. A sci-fi adventure caper set in the fortieth century, crammed with gadgets (a very 60s trend), camp dialogue and featuring immense psychedelic sets, it is a highly rated period piece and deserves mention in this account despite its lack of any obvious UK film or music connection.

Jane Fonda and Michel Piccoli

Released 22 June 1966, 98 minutes, colour
DVD: released by Fox Lorber, 23 September 2003
SOUNDTRACK: vinyl release in the US on Atco in 1967

GEORGY GIRL

Silvio Narizzano directs
Lynn Redgrave, Charlotte Rampling
and Alan Bates star

Lynn Redgrave

A four-way study of sexual politics that was considered very frank in 66, *Georgy Girl* starred Lynn Redgrave, James Mason, Alan Bates and Charlotte Rampling. Directed by Silvio Narizzano from a script by Peter Nichols (who had written the Dave Clark Five vehicle *Catch Us If You Can*), the plot revolves around Redgrave rebuffing the attentions of both Bates and Mason and eventually being left with the job of bringing up her friend's unwanted baby.

Produced by Columbia Pictures, as in *Alfie* the action is filmed around London and, like that film, *Georgy Girl* also enjoyed an enormous box office success, particularly in the US where it was one of the top ten money-making films of the time and was nominated for four Academy Awards. Premiered at the Berlin Film Festival in June 66, it was released in the US prior to reaching the cinemas in the UK, possibly because of the impact *Alfie* had made a few months earlier.

The film boasted a breezy and very commercial title song, written by Tom Springfield and 50s coffee bar pop actor Jim Dale. Performed by The Seekers, it charted at number two in the US and number three in the UK being played (and heard) so frequently that it quickly became part of the wallpaper of the decade. A subsequent *Georgy Girl* US LP by The Seekers – unrelated to the film – reached number ten. The remainder of the soundtrack, which includes an uncredited contribution from pop-psych group The Mirage, was produced by Alexander Faris, who went on to arrange the seminal Al Stewart LP *'Bedsitter Images'* a year later, a work that dealt with some of the same themes explored by the film.

Released 17 October 1966, 99 minutes, black and white
DVD: released by UCA, May 2005
SOUNDTRACK: No official release

In the Land of the Auteurs

Despite the stylistic debt owed by Swinging London to French and Italian *auteurs*, a comparable genre based in Paris or Rome failed to emerge. Although the huge array of balladeers, popular orchestras and homely MOR entertainers who packed out the charts of Europe throughout the 60s and 70s frequently appeared in films, few were anything other than the local equivalent of Cliff Richard features: musical comedies, school comedies, romantic comedies, comedies of all types. But there were exceptions…

Hurra die Rattles Kommen! (66) showcased German stars The Rattles, supported by The Liverbirds and Casey Jones and the Governors, the latter UK acts with bigger reputations in Hamburg than Merseyside. Further north in Finland, The Renegades, from Birmingham, featured in *Topralli*, whilst the Belgian TV special *Ram-Jam* (also 66) had Dusty Springfield, The Golden Earrings, The Frugal Sound and Neil Landon and the Italian feature *La Battaglia dei Mods/The Battle of the Mods* starred German star Ricky Shayne, Austrian balladeer Udo Jürgens and Donovan in a caper about mods and

rockers in Liverpool. With hindsight, it is hardly surprising that continental popsters tended to appear in film genres that were typical of their home country.

The French penchant for crime dramas brought Françoise Hardy in *Une balle au coeur/Devil at My Heels* (66), Adamo in *Les Arnauds/The Arnauds* (67) and *L'Ardoise/The Comeuppance* (70) and Johnny Hallyday in *À Tout Casser/The Great Chase* (68) and *Point de Chute* (70). In Italy spaghetti westerns featured Rita Pavone in *Little Rita nel West/Crazy Westerners* and *La Feldmarescialla* (both 67), Bobby Solo doing the main theme for *Per mille dollari al Giorno/ For One Thousand Dollars Per Day* (67) and Johnny Hallyday (again) in *Gli Specialisti/The Specialists* (69). Spanish hit act Los Bravos appeared in two inane musical comedies: *Los Chicos con Las Chicas/The Boys and The Girls* (67) and *Dame un poco de amor/Give me a Little Love* (68) – the latter the more interesting piece … a sci-fi adventure in the style of *The Monkees* TV series with the group performing material written by Vanda and Young of The

Easybeats. Their lead singer, Mike Kennedy (aka Michael Kögel), later had a significant solo career during which he appeared in the 71 Italian thriller shot in London, *A Lizard in a Woman's Skin*, as 'hippy guy', some way down a cast headed by Stanley Baker. Elsewhere *Le Cerveau/The Brain* (69) was an international crime caper with scenes shot in Carnaby Street and a title theme by Caterina Caselli whilst *Le Champignon/The Mushroom* (70) starred Mylène Demongeot from *Bonjour Tristesse* and boasted a soundtrack by French jazz-rockers Zoo.

Although neither pop nor rock, the huge success of Ennio Morricone's soundtrack LP for *Il buono, il brutto, il cattivo/The Good, The Bad and The Ugly* (number two in the UK charts in late 68) reflected the popularity of Euro orchestras and their conductors, many of whom worked as frequently in their own countries as John Barry did in the UK and US. Bert Kaempfert scored *You Can't Win 'Em All* (70) a sprawling comedy war film, Marcello Minerbi did the spaghetti western *Una pistola per cento croci/Gunman of One Hundred*

Crosses (71) whilst Paul Mauriat (who hit the UK singles charts with *'Love is Blue'* in early 68 covered successfully and bizarrely by Jeff Beck) did the music for the horror fantasy *Lisa e il diavolo/Lisa and The Devil* (73). Perhaps the most interesting of all was Argentine conductor Waldo de los Rios who produced the soundtracks for *La residencia/The House That Screamed* (69), a horror film starring John Moulder-Brown (later seen in *Deep End*), the Spanish pop film *A 45 Revoluciones por Minuto* with Formula V and Los Angeles, and the spaghetti westerns *Una città chiamata bastarda/A Town Called Hell* and *El hombre de Rio Malo/Bad Man's River* (both 71). A typical feature of many MOR Euro orchestra soundtracks was the compression of a wide range of musical styles into a single LP: *faux* opera, stark, minimalist and almost avant garde modern classical, Shadows-style pop, hard rock and big ballads all jostling for position on the same piece of vinyl.

The difficulties that afflicted the UK film industry in the 70s were not nearly as apparent

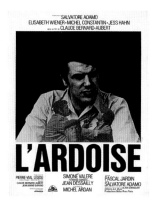

in France, Germany and Italy where, sustained by significant government subsidies for the performing arts, large numbers of feature films continued to be made for the domestic market. This was true even with exploitation genres, such as horror and sex, where the (by UK standards) explicit attitude towards nudity and violence produced *Sapho ou la fureur d'aimer/Sex is my Game* (71) with a theme song by David Alexandre Winter, the German TV production *Vampira* (71) with music from Tangerine Dream (who also scored *Geradeaus bis zum Morgen/Straight Ahead 'til Morning* in 72), Michel Delpech's soundtrack for *Le rampart des Beguines/The Beguines* (72) and Giorgio Moroder's music for *Die Klosterschülerinnen/Sex Life in a Convent* (72). Germany, in particular, was fertile ground for film opportunities for rock bands: Amon Düül II were used by Fassbinder in *The Niklashausen Journey* and by Syberberg in San Domingo

(both 70) and also contributed to the Israeli co-production *Chamsin* (72) reckoned by some to be a late psychedelic masterpiece; Can scored *Kamasutra – Vollendung der Liebe* (69), *The Brutes* (70) and *Secret Life of a Schoolgirl Wife* (71)… with these and *Deep End*, and many more outside this period, they come a close second to Pink Floyd in their number of film and TV appearances; Birth Control and Murphy Blend both turn up in *Ich-Eine Groupie/Higher and Higher* (70). In Europe, serious mainstream drama such as Godard's *Tout va bien/That's Great* (72) automatically came with music from the latest pop/rock artists, in this instance Stone and Charden. It was very different in the UK where, by 74, the film industry had no use for the latest pop artists – Sweet, Mott the Hoople, David Bowie, Roxy Music – whilst, beyond Calais, any pop or rock star wanting a career in front of the camera was guaranteed a lengthy string of screen credits.

CHARLIE IS MY DARLING

Peter Whitehead directs
The Rolling Stones star

Charlie Watts does the honours for a fan

The huge success of The Beatles' first two films appears to have convinced Andrew Loog Oldham, manager of The Rolling Stones, that his charges too should have a celluloid outing, especially as their massive global hit in the summer of 65 with *'I Can't Get No Satisfaction'* seemed to confirm their international standing as an antidote to the mainstream wackiness of the Fab Four. Oldham commissioned documentary maker and cameraman Peter Whitehead – best known at this point for *Wholly Communion*, a film of an Allen Ginsberg poetry festival at the Albert Hall – to shoot some live performances by The Rolling Stones in Dublin in September 65. These were then intercut with interviews with the group members and *cinéma verité* footage of the band relaxing offstage and on their travels.

Although completed and ready for release, rather surprisingly the film was shelved, apart from a screening at the Mannheim Film Festival in October 66. One wonders why this was so. Were the reasons mundane? At that point, no one had released a feature showing a band in concert. What if it failed? By the time DA Pennebaker proved the potential of the genre with *Dont Look Back* and *Monterey Pop* in 67-68, the footage in *Charlie is my Darling* may already have been considered a bit old hat, and the exit of Brian Jones from the group in 69 would have finally consigned it to the archives. Peter Whitehead went on to make the fondly regarded documentary *Tonite Let's All Make Love in London*, whilst The Rolling Stones finally made their screen debut (discounting some footage of them in the 64 US concert film *The T.A.M.I. Show*) in Jean-Luc Godard's *Sympathy for the Devil*, nearly three years later.

Barely a footnote in cinema reference books for forty years, the film was finally released to some acclaim in September 2012.

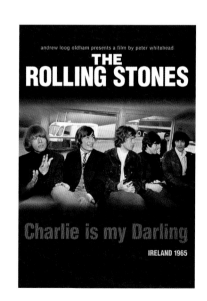

Released October 1966, 60 minutes, black and white
DVD: available November 2012 via ABKCO Films
SOUNDTRACK: no release, integral with film

Mick and the Droogs?

Looking for a film for The Rolling Stones that would be as outrageous as possible (and therefore trump The Beatles), their manager, Andrew Loog Oldham, attempted as early as 64 to option Anthony Burgess's book *A Clockwork Orange*, imagining the group members playing the central roles of Alex and his gang in this account of a violently dystopian future. He failed but, a year later, June 65, Andy Warhol released *Vinyl*, his 'adaptation' of the book, filmed unrehearsed in his studio in New York, with an unknown cast and, curiously, a pop soundtrack that included The Rolling Stones' *'The Last Time'*. Reviews were poor (excepting the art press), distribution was non-existent and, predictably, it played to a miniscule audience. Oldham's interest revived, though, and via Michael Cooper, court photographer to the Stones and a key figure in their *entourage*, Terry Southern was told about the book and the interest in it being a vehicle for Oldham's charges. At this point one of the highest paid screen writers in the world, Southern had met Warhol at the 66 Cannes Film Festival, where Warhol had been promoting his work. He optioned the book and did a script that starred Jagger with the other Rolling Stones as gang members. Michael Cooper was proposed as director. Even in the balmy days of the mid-late 60s, securing funding for a project with no acting stars and no 'name' director proved tricky and a later version had David Hemmings in the key role, Jagger a possible co-star, and Richard Lester tentatively at the helm. Further problems arose when the Lord Chamberlain (to whom the script had to be submitted, as the final arbiter of what was permissible in UK film, stage and TV) promptly advised that it would be banned because of explicit content. Southern's option lapsed without the project moving forward. The idea failed to die, though. Southern told Stanley Kubrick about the book and after censorship was relaxed in the UK (late 68, exit the Lord Chamberlain) Kubrick optioned the book and shot it in 70-71 with Malcolm McDowell in the main role after seeing him in *If...*

The Lester + Southern + Hemmings + Jagger version of *A Clockwork Orange* remains one of the great 'what ifs' of film history and Jagger had to wait until *Performance* to play a leading role: in another film that explored delinquency and violence.

David Hemmings at work

BLOW-UP

Michelangelo Antonioni directs
David Hemmings stars

Possibly the outstanding example of the 60s British pop film, *Blow-Up* was a major studio picture, funded by MGM, produced by Carlo Ponti and directed by Italian *auteur* Michelangelo Antonioni. Filmed in Notting Hill Gate and a variety of representative London settings (Peckham, Greenwich, Stockwell), it takes a disenchanted view of London as the centre of the pop world, presenting much of it as an empty materialistic phenomenon in a manner not dissimilar to that presented by Fellini in *La Dolce Vita*. After it had been turned down by Terence Stamp, the main role was taken by David Hemmings – up until then a minor figure in UK films – but, after the success of *Blow-Up*, a major box office draw for

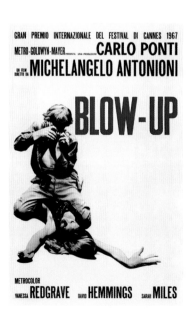

the rest of the decade. He plays a fashion photographer who thinks he may have unwittingly witnessed a murder. Quite brilliant in parts, one sequence features top model Veruschka, with the film making the point that celebrity culture is hollow, posing questions about the nature of illusion and reality and with the twists and turns of the plot mocking the maxim that the camera never lies. Sarah Miles and Vanessa Redgrave co-starred and the film achieved some notoriety for an extended full frontal sex scene involving Hemmings, Jane Birkin and Gillian Hills. Hills was an actress with an established pop singing career in France. Birkin, of course, later followed a similar path.

Antonioni and Herbie Hancock, who did the soundtrack, wanted to include some shots of typical London/UK pop music of the time and considered using a number of acts including Eric Burdon (who turned it down, The Animals having just split), The In Crowd, Five's Company and The Velvet Underground (who were signed to MGM and available, but too expensive to bring across from New York). Realising that having a bankable and successful pop group on board would increase the film's box office performance, Antonioni eventually selected The Yardbirds, whose line up at this point included both Jimmy Page and Jeff Beck. They appear in a scene in which Hemmings wanders into a club where the initially catatonic audience, within which both Michael Palin and Janet Street-Porter can be momentarily glimpsed, explodes into a riot when Beck begins smashing up his guitar.

Blow-Up was a hugely successful film. The soundtrack (which includes The Yardbirds performing their set opener 'Stroll On') also sold well, reaching number one hundred and ninety seven in the US Album charts in May 67, a rare event at a time when soundtrack LPs were usually represented by Walt Disney spin-offs and Broadway cast recordings. When re-issued on EMI in 96 the soundtrack included two additional tracks (one entitled 'Blow- Up') credited to Tomorrow, the group that The In Crowd evolved into in late 66.

Released 18 December 1966, 111 minutes, colour
DVD: released by Warner Home Video, 2004
SOUNDTRACK: LP released by MGM (1966), CD reissue on EMI (1996)

THE FAMILY WAY

The Boulting brothers direct and produce
Hywel Bennett and Hayley Mills star

With a solid reputation in UK cinema dating back to the 40s (with social and political dramas such as *Brighton Rock* and *Fame is the Spur*) and 50s (when they produced anti-establishment comedies like *Lucky Jim* and *I'm Alright Jack*), the Boulting Brothers made a distinct play for the fashionable youth/pop market in the mid 60s. Their first attempt at this, *The Family Way*, was clearly a hangover from the earlier 'kitchen sink' genre, having begun life in 61 as the stage and radio play *All in Good Time*.

Written by Bill Naughton, at that point basking in the huge international success of *Alfie*, its plot was simple: a newly married couple who for one reason or another – embarrassment at peer pressure, the practicalities of intimacy whilst living in the spare bedroom in a tiny terraced house – cannot consummate their marriage. Filmed in and around Bolton (Naughton's home town) in the late summer of 66, the lead roles were taken by Hayley Mills, whose most striking part prior to this had been as a fifteen year old in the Northern drama *Whistle Down the Wind*, and Hywel Bennett, breathtakingly known as 'the new Burton'. An interesting supporting slot, sixth in the cast, was played by Murray Head, a young actor and aspiring Donovan-style folk singer who, during the 60s, released a range of material on the EMI/Columbia and Immediate labels, sang the lead part on the original 69 *Jesus Christ Superstar* concept album, before finally reaching film stardom in 71 with *Sunday Bloody Sunday*. He gets to perform in *The Family Way*, one of the tracks, '*Someday Soon*', subsequently being released as a single.

The Family Way soundtrack, by Paul McCartney and The George Martin Orchestra, included the main film theme '*Love in the Open Air*'. A version of this by The Tudor Minstrels was duly released as a single in December 66 but failed to sell. Nor, rather curiously, did the soundtrack LP, despite the involvement of McCartney (this is regarded by some as his first solo effort) and the vast sales that usually attended anything Beatle connected at this time. *The Family Way* was a considerable box office success in the UK but ran into censorship problems in the US due to a very brief, almost chaste, nude scene.

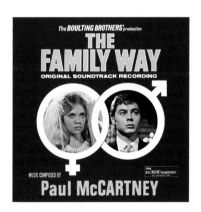

Released December 1966,
115 minutes, colour
DVD: Released June 2003
by Elevation as part of The Boulting
Brothers Collection
SOUNDTRACK: LP issued on Decca
in 1967. CD reissued in 1996

Marianne Faithfull

ANNA

Anna Karina stars
Serge Gainsbourg does the music

Like *The Game is Over* and *La Collectionneuse*, *Anna* is an example of a 60s European film aimed squarely at the burgeoning youth market. Like them, it also provides a significant role for a rising UK pop celebrity: in this case Marianne Faithfull, Decca recording star and girlfriend of Mick Jagger, making her second appearance in a major art movie after her cameo in Godard's *Made in U.S.A.*

A pop comedy/musical devised by Serge Gainsbourg, *Anna* was the first major colour production made for French TV. Directed by Pierre Koralnik (who would later work with Gainsbourg on *Cannabis*) it starred Anna Karina, the wife of Jean-Luc Godard who, a few years later, would be seen in such trippy entertainments as *The Magus* and *Justine*. The plot, which in some ways echoes that of *Blow-Up*, concerns a man who is so struck by a fleeting glimpse of an image of a woman in a photograph that he searches the length and breadth of Paris trying to find her.

As well as appearing in a co-starring role, Gainsbourg wrote the film's music, displaying, even at this early stage, an extraordinary mastery of UK pop styles. This is especially evident in the scene where Karina performs 'Roller Girl' (a major French pop hit of the time) and the sequence where Faithfull drifts through a crowd singing 'Hier ou Demain', the latter, not, however, included on the soundtrack LP.

BROADCAST: 13 January 1967,
87 minutes, colour
DVD: reissued by Mercury, 2009
SOUNDTRACK: LP issued on Philips,
1967. CD issued by Mercury, 2009

JUST LIKE A WOMAN

Robert Fuest directs
Wendy Craig and Francis Matthews star

A small but perfectly formed example of all the ingredients that went together to make up a typical Swinging London film, *Just Like a Woman* resembles a cross between an upmarket TV commercial and a trailer for the Ideal Home Exhibition. It opens with a brilliantly inventive title sequence – from Derek Nice, who later created *Arnold Layne*, the three minute promotional short for the debut Pink Floyd single – that mixes pop art, Victoriana and cool jazz and was the directorial debut of Robert Fuest, previously production designer on the first *Avengers* TV series in 61-62.

A comedy of manners about the various tribulations in the marriage of a television producer the film is both modish and visual. The cast is led by Wendy Craig, previously in *The Servant*, and Francis Matthews, just at that point becoming 'noticed' after much TV work and a couple of co-starring roles in Hammer horrors. Matthews, in fact, did quite a bit of pop work during this period: including a major voiceover role in *Captain Scarlet and the Mysterons*, one of many hugely successful puppet series at this time, that also featured music from The Spectrum, and the lead in *Paul Temple*, a TV series about an elegant jet-setting detective. Some way down the bill, in a supporting role, is Barry Fantoni who, as well as taking acting jobs, was the presenter of *A Whole Scene Going*, the first TV magazine show for teenagers combining music, fashion and much else. Fantoni was quite a figure at this time: a founder member of the satirical magazine *Private Eye* who also angled for a career of his own as a pop star. He had a couple of singles out on Fontana whilst filming *Just Like a Woman*, one of which, '*Little Man in a Little Box*', was written by Ray Davies of The Kinks.

An interesting curio is it was scored by Kenny Napper, bass player in the Johnny Dankworth Band, who had previously done the music for *All Night Long*, the 62 film that set *Othello* in a Soho jazz club and starred Patrick McGoohan, Dankworth, Dave Brubeck, Tubby Hayes and many others. Here the soundtrack, demonstrating that Swinging London was by no means entirely dependent on pop, and included much jazz as well, features vocalist Mark Murphy, who also appears at several points in the film, and whose output at this time, on Fontana and Immediate, is now highly collectable.

Released 26 February 1967, 89 minutes, colour
DVD: available from Digital Classics, 2009
SOUNDTRACK: None released

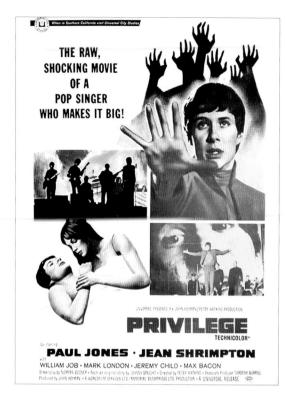

PRIVILEGE

Paul Jones stars, from a script by Johnny Speight

Co-produced by Albert Finney, *Privilege* was the first feature directed by Peter Watkins, who began working on it after winning an Academy Award for *The War Game*, the celebrated (and banned) 65 documentary/drama about the horrors of a nuclear attack on Britain. Like *The War Game*, the tone of *Privilege* was deadly serious, even to the point of being slightly hysterical. The plot, from a script by Johnny Speight, postulates that 'in the near future' (presumably the early 70s) the UK government will cynically control young people by creating superficial pop stars whose mass popularity is cultivated and subverted by them within a quasi-religious setting akin to that of Mary Whitehouse and the Festival of Light.

The film starred Paul Jones, who gave an earnest performance, and contemporary supermodel Jean Shrimpton. The popularity of Jones, lead singer of Manfred Mann until a few months previously, ensured good box office, this being duly reflected in the sales of his solo single *'I've been a bad bad boy'* (a song featured in the film) which reached number five in the charts and an EP *'Songs from Privilege'* which reached number one in its chart and sold consistently well throughout 67.

The soundtrack LP was produced by Mike Leander and included a contribution from the group George Bean and the Runners who also appear briefly in the film.

Released 28 February 1967, 103 minutes, colour
DVD: re-issued by BFI in 2009
SOUNDTRACK: LP issued in 1967

LA COLLECTIONNEUSE

Eric Rohmer directs
Giorgio Gomelsky does the music

The first Eric Rohmer film to be widely seen outside France – and certainly the first to make any impact in the UK – *La Collectionneuse* starred Haydée Politoff as a young woman who decides to experiment by having a different boyfriend every day. Much of the action takes place in St Tropez, with a louche supporting cast that includes Donald Cammell, a one time society painter and a quintessential figure in Swinging London UK cinema with a string of credits that would later include *Duffy*, *The Touchables* and *Performance*.

The pop connection in the film came when producer Barbet Schroeder, who would later direct *More* and *La Vallée*, asked French-Georgian music impresario Giorgio Gomelsky to supervise the soundtrack. Gomelsky hired his protégés The Ingoes – an English pop and r'n'b group unknown in their home country but with a degree of popularity in France – to play much of the music. Their guitarist Brian Belshaw also has an uncredited role as one of Ms Politoff's many male friends.

By the time the film was released across Europe (where it won the Special Jury Prize at the Berlin Film Festival), Gomelsky had decamped to the UK, taking The Ingoes with him where, as Blossom Toes, they became an important part of the burgeoning psychedelic scene.

Haydée Politoff with Patrick Bachau

Released March 1967, 89 minutes, colour
DVD: released by Fusion Media Sales in October 2010 as part of The Eric Rohmer Collection
SOUNDTRACK CD/LP: uncertain. A CD by The Ingoes, *'Before we were Blossom Toes'*, was released in 2010 on Sunbeam and may contain material used in the film

MORD UND TOTSCHLAG
(A DEGREE OF MURDER)

Volker Schlöndorff directs
Anita Pallenberg stars
Brian Jones does the music

The second feature directed by West German auteur Volker Schlöndorff, *Mord und Totschlag*, was filmed in late 66 and premiered at the Cannes Film Festival in April 67. Starring Anita Pallenberg, the plot is about the careless murder of a young man by his girlfriend and the conspiracy that follows to cover this up and dispose of his body. The general amorality of the characters (and some casual sex) made it a popular film in the nascent counter-culture of its time, particularly in Europe, but it only received a limited release elsewhere.

The clearly observed multi-instrumental accomplishments of the Rolling Stones' Brian Jones, heard on tracks like *'Under My Thumb'* and *'Dandelion'* at this time, and the fact that he was Pallenberg's boyfriend, led to him getting the job of composing the music for the film's soundtrack. He was assisted by Jimmy Page (then in The Yardbirds), Nicky Hopkins, Kenney Jones (The Small Faces) and Peter Gosling (a minor figure in The Rolling Stones entourage, who co-wrote, with Bill Wyman, material recorded by The End).

Sadly, 'due to copyright reasons', there was no formal release for the material he painstakingly worked on for six months in somewhat difficult personal circumstances; and by the time the film eventually appeared in the US (where it was shown to coincide with The Rolling Stones 69 tour), Jones had both left the group and been found drowned in his swimming pool.

Hans Peter Hallwachs and Anita Pallenberg

Released April 1967, 87 minutes, colour
DVD: unofficial release by Pignon Music Video
CD: no formal release

JEU DE MASSACRE

Alain Jessua directs
Guy Peellaert draws the cartoons

A French production shot in late 66 and early 67 by Alain Jessua, a lesser known *auteur*, *Jeu de Massacre* marries very Mod faux pop art sets and design with an absurd quasi James Bond plot in which a feckless playboy hires two cartoonists to draw a series of adventures featuring himself. The French – and Belgian – interest in graphic art had been reflected on film and TV for many years, particularly via the popular *Tintin* series broadcast from 59 onwards, whilst the frantic mix of espionage and skullduggery underpinning this had already been seen in films like the 64 Jean-Paul Belmondo vehicle *That Man From Rio*.

Claudine Auger comforts her co-star Jean-Pierre Cassel

The title sequence here, and much of the other graphic imagery used in the production, was drawn by Guy Peellaert who later achieved worldwide success in 73 as the co-author of *Rock Dreams* and, following on from this, became a much sought after designer of LP sleeves. *Jeu de Massacre* (*The Killing Game* in the UK and US) was a major production that premiered at the Cannes Film Festival in April 67, where it won a prize for best script. The leading roles were played by Michel Duchaussoy, Jean-Pierre Cassel and Claudine Auger, the latter a former Miss France who had just appeared with Sean Connery in *Thunderball*. France based US soul singer Nancy Holloway can also be seen in a supporting role. The film makes for an interesting comparison with *Modesty Blaise*, a somewhat more staid UK production seen in cinemas at around the same time.

The theme song is performed by The Alan Bown Set and got a release in France on Vogue. Bown (and several of his group) had formerly been members of The John Barry Seven, evolving out of that group when first Barry, and later Les Reed, departed to undertake film and TV work.

Released April 1967, 90 minutes, colour
DVD: French language version released on Studio Canal in 2004
SOUNDTRACK: CD re-issue on Vogue in 2001. EP release in 1967

Barry, Reed and Bown

Strictly speaking, John Barry predated pop. After national service in Egypt, he did arrangements for Jack Parnell and Ted Heath, leaders of the main UK big bands of the day, before leading his own combo in their matching purple suits through the dance halls and TV studies of 50s Britain. His ascent from this level of modest success came down to two lucky breaks: (1) In 59 he copied Dick Jacobs' arrangement of Buddy Holly's *'It Doesn't Matter Anymore'* for *'What Do You Want'*, the fourth single released by Adam Faith (the previous three had all tanked) and had an immediate mega hit – with many sequels as Faith became one of the biggest pop stars of the time – and inevitably gravitated to film work in a string of mainly dud movies… *Never Let Go*, *Mix Me a Person*, *The Cool Mikado*, *It's All Happening*, renamed *The Dream Maker*, (though, to be fair, he also did *Beat Girl*, renamed *Wild for Kicks*, and *The L-Shaped Room*); and (2) In 62 he had a hit of his own with a cover of Monty Norman's big band/lounge *'James Bond Theme'* from *Dr No* and became so identified with it that, following the surprising success of the film in the US (where by the end of the decade he had won three Academy Awards), he was hauled on board to do all the subsequent 007 soundtracks.

Within a very short while, Barry was effortlessly big time – sharing a flat with Michael Caine, cruising around London in an E-type Jag and producing a string of big US chart hits for the oh-so-English duo Chad and Jeremy. After meeting her on the set of *The Knack*, he married Jane Birkin (divorced 67)… the first of several much younger wives and girlfriends, the procession of which earned him the Byronesque epithet of being mad, bad and dangerous to know.

Where Barry trod, his erstwhile colleagues followed. Les Reed, piano player in The John Barry Seven, went solo and emerged as one of the biggest songwriters in mainstream UK pop, with a string of stratospherically successful hits for The Applejacks, The Fortunes, The Dave Clark Five, Tom Jones (*'It's Not Unusual'* *'Delilah'*), Paul and Barry Ryan, Lulu, PJ Proby, Petula Clark, Herman's Hermits and Engelbert Humperdinck (*'The Last Waltz'*). In 68 Decca gave him his own label – Chapter One. Yes… it was very MORish, but it also released gems by Episode Six, Toe Fat, The Californians and The March Hare. Reed, too, moved into films, initially with Ronan O'Rahilly's *The Girl on a Motorcycle*, later with *One More Time*, a Rat Pack spin-off set in Swinging London,

The John Barry Seven

and Crossplot the 69 Roger Moore dry run for the Bond role. His finest hour? 'Man of Action' – the theme music for Radio North Sea International, the pirate station that kept independent commercial radio alive on the airwaves in the early 70s.

And through it all, the band kept playing. In 64, Barry relinquished the leadership of his group to trumpeter Alan Bown who quickly rebranded them as The Alan Bown Set, purveying mod soul/pop/jazz/rock to the UK club and campus

scene for the next ten years. As well as Jeu de Massacre, they appeared in a 68 Jack Good Yorkshire TV Special alongside Julie Driscoll, Brian Auger and The Trinity, Lulu, The Flirtations and The Chants and eventually signed off with the theme for the 74 TV series The Rockford Files.

It's intriguing how much of the musical and cultural tapestry of the 60s came out of one group that played the UK ballroom circuit a decade earlier...

THE JOKERS

Michael Winner directs
Michael Crawford and Oliver Reed star

Despite his later proclivities with the *Death Wish* franchise, Michael Winner — originally a journalist with *The New Musical Express* — began his directing career with a number of enjoyable and deftly handled UK pop films including the Billy Fury vehicle *Play it Cool* and the trad jazz era kitchen sink drama *West Eleven*.

The Jokers, a big studio picture produced by Universal, is an engaging and entertaining example of his output during this time. With an excellent script by Dick Clement and Ian La Frenais, then basking in critical acclaim from their TV series *The Likely Lads*, it features Oliver Reed and Michael Crawford as two brothers whose escapades and scheming culminate in an attempt to steal (borrow?) the Crown Jewels. As was typical with most UK films of this period, the supporting cast and ensemble playing was strong thanks to the presence of Harry Andrews, Edward Fox, Rachel Kempson, Warren Mitchell, Frank Finlay and Michael Hordern. The filming locations weren't bad either… with shooting taking place in the Old Bailey, the Tower of London, posh bits of Kensington, various nightclubs, the now defunct Society Restaurant (a favoured haunt of, among others, the Kray brothers and Robin Douglas-Home, nephew of Alec and one time boyfriend of Princess Margaret) and at the Trooping of the Colour whilst Reed and Crawford career around in a Mini Moke. The 'Swinging London' ethos is firmly cemented with newsreel footage of Harold Wilson and Edward Heath being inserted into the narrative.

The film theme, 'The Jokers', by Peter and Gordon was subsequently released as a single — providing them with a minor hit in the US. The remainder of the soundtrack was composed by Johnny Pearson who did Cilla Black's arrangements as well as fronting his own outfit, Sounds Orchestral, a studio band that specialised in pastiche instrumentals and covers of pop hits.

Released 5 May 1967, 94 minutes, colour
DVD: Various reissues
SOUNDTRACK: No release

Crawford and Reed

SMASHING TIME

Rita Tushingham, Lynn Redgrave and Michael York star
in a George Melly script

Rita Tushingham protesting

By 67, major US studios were queuing up to produce films set in Swinging London. Paramount funded *Smashing Time*, which broadly speaking used the same plot as *A Hard Day's Night*: the central characters (Brenda and Yvonne) escape from the limitations of, 'the North' to sample the boundless possibilities on offer in the metropolis. With a sharply satirical script, written by jazz vocalist and *Observer* film critic George Melly, *Smashing Time* provides an excuse for various outings to London locations, culminating in an extended sequence in the revolving restaurant at the top of the Post Office Tower.

Directed by Desmond Davis – whose previous credits included an adaptation of Edna O'Brien's *Girl with Green Eyes* – the film starred Rita Tushingham and Lynn Redgrave with Michael York in the main supporting role. The struggling young actor/singer David Essex can also be glimpsed in a tiny part as a 'beatnik'. A particularly memorable sequence is set in a recording studio where Redgrave (as Yvonne) records a hit single *'I'm so young'* – a brilliantly overblown pastiche complete with sitar, brass section, strings etc.

Among the musicians backing her (and also appearing in the Post Office Tower finale) are the group Tomorrow, who, in a repetition of their involvement in *Blow-Up*, recorded material for the film that was not subsequently used. Also involved were Skip Bifferty, who are not seen on screen but can be heard performing various bits of incidental music.

Released 1967, 96 minutes, colour
DVD: available via Anchor Bay
SOUNDTRACK: released as an LP on Stateside in 67

Whatever Happened to the Battersea Bardot?

Diminutive, blonde hair, a lived-in face and a brooding, slightly haunted, hopeless look – Carol White's career followed the classic rags to riches and back again trajectory: a star at 17, a has-been at 30, and an early death amid the wreckage of drink, drugs and failed relationships.

First noticed as a St Trinian's schoolgirl and then elevated to parts in *Never Let Go* and *Beat Girl*, renamed *Wild for Kicks*, she had her first leading role in *Linda*, a 1960 film with a Joe Meek soundtrack, about teenage gangs in south London, that went out as the supporting feature to *Saturday Night and Sunday Morning*, but is now, alas, lost and unseen for decades. Instead of building on this, she chose marriage (to one of The King Brothers, a very tame English rock 'n' roll act of the time) and was promptly sidelined by having to raise two children. Her breakthrough came in a trio of glum dramas filmed in 65-67, *Up the Junction*, *Cathy*

Come Home (both for TV) and *Poor Cow*. After this Hollywood beckoned; but after co-starring in *Daddy's Gone-A Hunting* and *Something Big* – and an affair with Frank Sinatra – she was back in the UK for *The Man Who Had Power Over Women* (70), amid the machinations of the music industry, *Dulcima* (71) and *Made* (72) alongside guitarist and singer songwriter Roy Harper. *Some Call It Loving* (73) was her final leading role.

In the years that followed, her increasingly rare appearances included *The Squeeze* (77 – in trouble, again, in south London) and the original stage production of *Steaming* (81) but her death, at forty eight, a few years later was still a shock. Her iconic appearance was used by pop artist Guy Peellaert in one of his images in *Rock Dreams* – as Cathy, hopelessly pushing her pram along the grim streets of inner London, accompanied by Ray Davies, brilliant pop chronicler of the English traditional side of the 60s.

POOR COW

Ken Loach directs
Carol White and Terence Stamp star

Stamp and White

Before houses in London SW11 cost £2m each, the area hosted a triptych of grim, downbeat dramas looking at local working class life. Like *Cathy Come Home* and *Up the Junction*, *Poor Cow* focuses on the poor choices available to (and made) by a young woman, played by Carol White.

Co-starring Terence Stamp, appearing here in the polar opposite of the role he had been offered and turned down in *Alfie*, it was produced by Joseph Janni, one of the major UK industry figures of the time, whose credits included *A Kind of Loving* and *Billy Liar*. Ken Loach directed, his previous work having included the TV version of *Cathy Come Home* and numerous episodes of *Z Cars* – the latter a realistic and very popular police drama set on Merseyside. The supporting players reflected Loach's penchant for utilising otherwise unsung bit part actors and actresses (check out legendary theatrical subversive Ken Campbell, appearing here as Mr Jacks – ninth in the cast list) with several of the roles being handed to local people. John Bindon, billed third, was the most prominent of these, and very much the real ticket: a London gangster whose later career included marrying a society model, appearances in *Performance* and *Get Carter*, holidaying with Princess Margaret, touring the US with Led Zeppelin and being charged with murder. (He was acquitted).

The soundtrack deliberately underscores the ephemeral and universal appeal of pop music for the characters portrayed and boasts material by The Lovin' Spoonful; The New Vaudeville Band; Lesley Duncan; Dave Berry; The Flower Pot Men; The Rolling Stones; Peter and Gordon and The Pretty Things. Donovan did the title song, which was subsequently released on the b-side of his single *Jennifer Juniper* in February 68.

Released 1967, 101 minutes, colour
DVD: reissued by Optimum Releasing
SOUNDTRACK: No official release

HOW I WON THE WAR

Richard Lester directs
Michael Crawford and John Lennon star

An absurdist drama that is also well observed (and historically accurate in many details), *How I Won the War* presents a deeply anti-heroic view of the British military, openly mocking its class-ridden attitudes.

A return engagement for many of the team associated with *Help!*, it presents World War Two as a chaotic, Swinging and vaguely counter-culture event – rather like an early UK entry into the predominantly US genre that eventually included *The Dirty Dozen, Catch-22, Kelly's Heroes, MASH* and *Slaughterhouse-Five*. The script, by Charles Wood, is excellent and drawn from an acerbic and irreverent novel by Patrick Ryan, based on his semi-farcical war experiences. The film starred Michael Crawford as a simpleton stumbling through cataclysmic events, and, in a major coup, John Lennon (surprisingly good in deadpan fashion) who shot his sequences at about the same time The Beatles were working on Sergeant Pepper. Both are accompanied by a fine supporting cast, led by Roy Kinnear (a Lester regular), Michael Hordern and Jack MacGowran, later in *Wonderwall*.

Lennon did not appear on the soundtrack LP, but a single from it – the title song *'How I Won The War'* – was issued by Musketeer Gripweed (the character Lennon played in the film) and the Third Troop. Speculation continues as to whether or not he appears on the record.

John Lennon does his bit

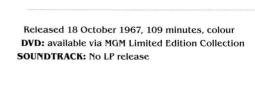

Released 18 October 1967, 109 minutes, colour
DVD: available via MGM Limited Edition Collection
SOUNDTRACK: No LP release

TO SIR, WITH LOVE

James Clavell directs
Sidney Poitier stars

One of the most popular films of its time, *To Sir, With Love* was an adaptation of the 59 ER Braithwaite novel about the tribulations of a black teacher, from the West Indies, in a tough school in the East End of London. Made by Columbia, it starred Sidney Poitier and was one of three films he appeared in at that time which tackled 'race' issues, the others being *In the Heat of the Night* and *Guess Who's Coming to Dinner*. A perfectly judged assault on the US market – there are extensive background shots of London buses, street markets etc – it was directed by James Clavell, a writer previously best known for his screenplays for *The Great Escape*, *633 Squadron* and *King Rat*, who had lived and worked in Hollywood some years previously.

The Mindbenders at the school dance

The main supporting roles are played by Christian Roberts, Judy Geeson and Suzy Kendall as mildly delinquent teenagers. The film was a great success in the UK and a massive hit in the US – where it made Poitier (briefly) the number one box office draw. Its central plot – a new teacher having difficulty imposing himself on unruly working class youths – was recycled and used in the 68 London Weekend TV series *Please Sir*, where it was played for comedy and the race element dropped. The original film even spawned a sequel: *To Sir, With Love II*, directed by Peter Bogdanovich in 96 with Poitier and Geeson reprising their earlier roles.

The soundtrack was supervised by Mike Leander and, when released as an LP, reached number twenty four in the US. The film includes performances from The Mindbenders and Lulu. The latter's rendition of the title song reached no 1 in the US as well as charting in a number of other territories though not, strangely, in the UK.

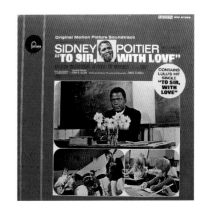

Released 29 October 1967, 105 minutes, colour
DVD: available from Columbia Tristar in 2000
SOUNDTRACK: released on Fontana in 1967

THE MINI AFFAIR

Robert Amram directs
Georgie Fame stars

A rare directing job for US documentary maker Robert Amram (who cut his teeth writing the script for the 64 UK short *Mods and Rockers*, which, among other things, contrasted the musical styles of The Cheynes and Heinz) *The Mini-Affair* was filmed in London in the spring of 67.

The plot – which was rendered implausible by the film's prologue subsequently being removed from the release prints – concerns a group of teenage girls who kidnap the men of their dreams … a pop star, a pirate radio DJ and a cabinet minister(!) … so that they can marry them.

The starring role, of the pop star, was played by Georgie Fame in his only known acting appearance. Considerable hopes were pinned on the film soundtrack. This included material written by Alan Blaikley and Ken Howard, then enjoying success with The Herd, and a clutch of songs specially commissioned from the Gibb brothers. These are performed by Fame (who sings '*Words*', later a huge hit for The Bee Gees) and The Majority, one of the less well known groups of the period, who appear singing another Gibb brothers composition '*All My Christmases*'.

The Mini-Affair had a limited release, appearing in the UK in late 67 and in the US from May 68, where it was known as *The Mini-Mob*. Curiously, given the enormous popularity of Fame and The Bee Gees at this point, no formal soundtrack was released, although the film's musical director Bill Shepherd issued a US LP in 68 entitled *The Bill Shepherd Singers Sing Bee Gee Hits* – this perhaps being the only artefact associated with the film to reach a wider public.

Released 1967, 92 minutes, colour
DVD: Not available
SOUNDTRACK: Not available

TONITE LET'S ALL MAKE LOVE IN LONDON

Peter Whitehead directs
Andrew Loog Oldham does the music

The film that cemented the reputation of Peter Whitehead as an ultra-hip figure in UK cinema, *Tonite Let's All Make Love in London*, subtitled 'A Pop Concerto', is a freewheeling feature-length documentary in which many of the fashionable figures of Swinging London appear against a desperately contemporary musical backdrop.

Shot in 66 and 67, and funded by the National Film Finance Corporation (the bank of last resort for serious uncommercial projects), the material includes footage of a riot at The Rolling Stones 66 Royal Albert Hall gig, glimpses of Julie Christie, Michael Caine, Edna O'Brien and Lee Marvin talking about sex, the original line up of Pink Floyd performing *'Interstellar Overdrive'*, and appearances by Allen Ginsberg and David Hockney. The tone is similar to an Attenborough or Dimbleby show: almost official, rather as if the era and its foibles were being endorsed by a *Guardian* style editorial.

For the soundtrack, Whitehead continued the relationship with Andrew 'Loog' Oldham (who appears here discussing his own future) that had started with *Charlie is my Darling*. Formally released on Oldham's Immediate subsidiary label Impact in July 68, it features The Small Faces, Chris Farlowe, Twice as Much, Vashti Bunyan and The Marquis of Kensington, the latter being the *nom de plume* of Robert Wace, one time manager of The Kinks.

Whitehead did not, though, develop a career in cinema along the lines of a Godard or a Herzog. After three further films over the following ten years, all semi-documentaries, none of which reached large audiences, he concentrated on writing.

Released November 1967, 72 minutes, black and white and colour
DVD: Double set issued by BFI 2007
SOUNDTRACK: LP released on Impact records July 1968, reissued on See For Miles 1990. CD reissues 1991 and 1999

HERE WE GO ROUND THE MULBERRY BUSH

Clive Donner directs
Judy Geeson stars

A big UK box office success and a fondly regarded film of its time, *Here We Go Round the Mulberry Bush* was filmed in Stevenage, one of the New Towns developed after 45 to provide housing and employment for people moving out of London. It was adapted from a novel by Hunter Davies who, a year earlier, had published *The New London Spy*, probably the first *Time Out*-style guide to fashionable venues and pursuits in the capital. Davies' novel described the sexual and emotional adventures of a young man growing-up in an idyllic, clean and modern environment surrounded by numerous, seemingly available teenage girls.

Directed by Clive Donner, whose previous credits included *The Caretaker*, *Nothing But the Best* and *What's New Pussycat?*, and produced by Larry Kramer (who would later enjoy a massive hit with *Women in Love*), the film was excessively youth-centric, and appeared to have no concept of life after twenty five. The BFI Monthly Film Bulletin commented at the time: "…The only incongruity is that it should have been made by adults so completely does it enter into the teenager's view of himself…" Given its overriding concern with sex, its use of comedy and suburban setting, there is a strong case for saying that it unwittingly served as the prototype of the later slew of 70s British sex films.

Starring Barry Evans and Judy Geeson, who in an echo of the above sentiment would both later be reunited in the decidedly inferior 76 film *Adventures of a Taxi Driver*, *Here We Go Round the Mulberry Bush* had an interesting soundtrack. Originally Hunter Davies approached Paul McCartney, on the back of *The Family Way*, to do the score. McCartney declined, but suggested that Davies write instead an authorised biography of The Beatles – which duly appeared in 68. The film's musical component was then entrusted to Simon Napier-Bell, previously producer of The Yardbirds, and ended up featuring material by The Spencer Davis Group, Traffic and Andy Ellison. The title song, released as a single by Traffic in November 67, reached number seven in the UK chart.

Released 1967, 96 minutes, colour
DVD: released by the BFI in 2009.
SOUNDTRACK: released as LP by United Artists in 1968, as CD by RPM in 1997

BEDAZZLED

Stanley Donen directs
Peter Cook and Dudley Moore star

An unusual teaming, by producers Twentieth Century Fox, of Hollywood great Stanley Donen, whose many credits included the musicals *On the Town* and *Singin' in the Rain*, with UK satirists Peter Cook and Dudley Moore, who wrote the screenplay and starred in what would turn out to be their only film venture of any substance.

Basically a modern version of the Faust legend, it co-stars Eleanor Bron (who had just appeared in *Alfie* and *Two for the Road*) and Raquel Welch, the latter a rising star after *One Million Years BC* and the faux Bond comedy *Fathom* (and who had originally risen to fame as a singer: see her appearance in the 65 beach party film *A Swingin' Summer*). Cook and Moore had wanted Julie Andrews (!) as the main female foil, but the megastar of *The Sound of Music* declined such a left field offer. The action takes place in typical Swinging London settings, including the Post Office Tower etc. Cook (as the Devil) grants Moore (an ineffectual little man) seven wishes: each results in a separate sketch. The end result is very entertaining and the supporting cast includes a pre-Edna Everage Barry Humphries.

Moore did the soundtrack, which includes a brilliant pop sequence where Moore performs a heavily orchestrated love song in the style of PJ Proby or Barry Ryan (i.e. over the top) and Cook replies – and trumps him – with a minimalist/existential number à la Scott Walker.

Released 10 December 1967, 103 minutes, colour
DVD: Released by Second Sight in July 2005
SOUNDTRACK: Released 1968 in the UK on Decca.
CD reissue on Harkit 2007

Raquel Welch in action with Dudley Moore

MAGICAL MYSTERY TOUR

The Beatles direct and star

The Beatles, post Pepper

For their third cinematic project, The Beatles dropped the discipline and framework of working with an established director (Richard Lester) and a major studio (United Artists) and opted instead for a series of sketches, with musical interludes, that they assembled themselves. A degree of supervision came from Bernard Knowles – who worked at Gainsborough Studios in the 40s and had later been involved in the popular ITV series *The Adventures of Robin Hood* in the 50s. What emerged from this collaboration wobbled between zany Goon Show absurdity and coy family entertainment.

Viewed by some as self-indulgent and having no discernible plot, *Magical Mystery Tour* was very much centred on The Beatles, in various disguises and costumes, though smaller roles were played by The Bonzo Dog Doo-Dah Band and even Ivor Cutler in a brief appearance. The film, like *Help!*, could accurately be described as a collection of music videos that had been stitched together and released for public consumption. Combining psychedelia with several showbizzy routines, it was apparently regarded at the time as suitable Christmas TV viewing for the family.

The accompanying soundtrack was produced by George Martin and included songs recorded between April and November 67, some of which had been discarded from the *Sgt. Pepper* project. One of these, 'I Am The Walrus', appeared as the b-side to 'Hello, Goodbye' and duly reached number one in most countries. The soundtrack LP was released on 27 November 67 and reached number one in the US, but only number thirty one in the UK, where it was followed by a double EP set (released on 8 December 67) which reached number two in the UK EP chart.

BROADCAST: 26 December 1967, 55 minutes, colour
DVD: released by MPI/Apple 1997
SOUNDTRACK: issued as LP by Parlophone 1967. Released as CD 1987

POPDOWN

Fred Marshall directs
Zoot Money stars
Giorgio Gomelsky does the music

Popdown was made by Fred Marshall, a US record producer with a string of easy listening albums to his credit, who pitched up in the UK in the mid 60s in the expectation he could profit by making something reflecting or including, no matter how loosely, the Swinging London phenomenon. Precisely what type of film Marshall made is still open to conjecture, particularly as the editing of the final product was so haphazard. Various versions of it have been seen and from the footage available, and the cast list, it appears to have been part music review, part circus review (a genre fashionable in the aftermath of *Sgt. Pepper*) and part nude review padded out with stock footage and bits of home movies with the result being released – kaleidoscope style with little dialogue – as a feature film.

The storyline in *Popdown* is simple, and daft: two aliens on a distant planet (played by Zoot Money, a noted character and musician on the London scene, and Jane Bates, a minor actress of the period) decide to investigate the pop culture on Planet Earth in the year 1970. Put this way the film resembles a survivor into the psychedelic era of the earlier rock and roll films of the 50s where an inane plot is used to link various often unrelated musical sequences. Filmed in early 68 and eventually costing £30,000 (£900k in current prices), an astonishingly high figure for such a simple project, it ran to 98 minutes as completed but was cut to a mere 45 minutes when eventually given a limited release, as a supporting feature, and already looking very dated in 70, ironically the year it was supposedly set. The main casualty of the trimming appears to have been the nude review section – Miss 1970, Nude on a camel, Nude in a Bubble, Miss Off key, Miss Off beat and Miss With It – much of which disappeared. The musical sequences are a fascinating time capsule and feature Kevin Westlake and Gary Farr, Blossom Toes, Julie Driscoll, Brian Auger and The Trinity and The Chris Barber Band from Giorgio Gomelsky's uber-hip Marmalade label, Zoot Money's group Dantallian's Chariot, The Idle Race, Andy Ellison, French-

Dantallion's Chariot

Canadian pop singer Nanette, Brazilian legend Luiz Bonfa and famed London busker Don Partridge. Lord Sitar (breathlessly thought to be George Harrison but subsequently revealed to be Big Jim Sullivan aka James Tomkins from Uxbridge, and the busiest session musician of the era) is heard in the background at one point sitaring his way through various pop hits of the period. The credits list no fewer than three different 'music producers': Tony Colton, who wrote Money's 66 hit *Big Time Operator*, Michel Hausser, an eminent French jazz vibraphonist who as part of the Orquesta Caravello had collaborated with Marshall on his easy listening LPs and John Hawkins who produced the Lord Sitar LP (as well as Cilla Black and The Locomotive), co-wrote the 66 instrumental *March of the Sky People* by The Galactic Federation and was later responsible for The Cape Kennedy Construction Company 69 single *The First Step on the Moon*… given how little we know now about *Popdown*, were either of these linked in some way to the film? The rapidity with which most of this roster faded away, and the ephemeral nature of the concept, is underlined in an obligatory discotheque sequence where we see (among many others) the writer Adam Diment dancing. Definitely a name to conjure with in 67/68, Diment was the acclaimed author of 'The Dolly Dolly Spy', the success of which led to it being announced as a film project by David Hemmings. Alas, it was never made and Diment didn't publish anything after 71.

Marshall was an elusive figure whose later film projects, which included a documentary for the Tahitian Tourist Board and productions in Hong Kong, Burma and the Philippines, were rarely screened outside occasional showings at film festivals. The full length version of *Popdown* has never been seen. One of the edited versions was last screened at the Scala Cinema, Kings Cross in 84 and a 25-minute version *Musicorama Popdown* briefly surfaced in 09. The film is not available in any format and no soundtrack LP was ever released.

Released 1970 (filmed early 1968), 45 minutes (cut from 98 minutes), colour
DVD: no release
SOUNDTRACK: no release

SEPARATION

Jack Bond directs
Jane Arden stars

Jane Arden was a significant figure in radical feminist theatre in the UK from the 50s through to the 70s, during which period she also worked on TV with Richard Lester and in theatre with Albert Finney. She stars in *Separation*, an intensely personal project, directed by Jack Bond whose later work would include a number of promotional films and videos for The Pet Shop Boys.

The plot concerns the life of a middle aged woman (played by Arden, who also wrote the script) after the break-up of her marriage. The film includes a sequence where she is subjected to intrusive analysis about her past by various male protagonists. In this respect it takes a similar view of psychiatry to that held by RD Laing – ultra fashionable in the counter-culture of the time – namely, that definitions of madness are often highly relative and made by people living outside the experiences being suffered by the victim. Ann Lynn, whose work included the beatnik drama *The Party's Over* with Oliver Reed, *Four in the Morning* and *Baby Love* co-stars.

A minor but effective mood piece, the psychedelic era is still present via costumes supplied by the boutique Granny Takes a Trip and the sound-track, which includes Procol Harum performing *'Salad Days'* – a track from their 67 debut album on Regal Zonophone – as well as some keyboard pieces by the band's Matthew Fisher, assisted by Cliff Barton, a sideman to Long John Baldry, Georgie Fame and Donovan, on bass.

Released 1968, 93 minutes, black and white
DVD: BFI release July 2009
SOUNDTRACK: No formal release

Sheila White and Peter Noone

MRS BROWN, YOU'VE GOT A LOVELY DAUGHTER

Allen Klein produces
Herman's Hermits star

Made by MGM as a starring vehicle for Peter Noone and Herman's Hermits, after their success in the vapid comedy *Hold On* (66), this production had a title song (originally performed by Tom Courtenay in the TV play *The Lads* in August 63) that had been a 65 US number one for them, during the four year period in which they came close to outselling The Beatles. The script, as written by Norman T Vane – who would later do *Twinky*, another US/ UK London based story – borrows freely from the template set by *A*

Hard Day's Night... opening with some grim shots of 60s Manchester ('the North') before the band relocate to London and become embroiled in an inane caper about the ownership of a racing greyhound. With Stanley Holloway, Mona Washbourne and Marjorie Rhodes co-starring, all stalwarts of British film comedies in the 40 and 50s, the end result, with its emphasis on song and dance, is not unlike *Mary Poppins* – a Disneyfied version of UK life for American audiences. It had originally been intended that Sandie Shaw would co-star. Her manager, however, turned down the part, preferring to accept instead a nebulous project in the south of France, due to be directed by Charles Gerard, that failed to materialise. Ms Shaw's role was taken by Sheila White, who put out two singles on CBS during this period and was later seen in *Here We Go Round the Mulberry Bush*.

Production duties were handled by Allen Klein, an aggressive and effective US impresario who offered his clients better financial arrangements than usually available elsewhere, at the expense of the longer term earnings/ownership of their catalogue. By early 67, he had replaced Andrew Loog Oldham as manager of The Rolling Stones and had also dipped a toe, successfully, into film production with the spaghetti western *A Dollar Between the Teeth*. He consolidated his position with *Mrs Brown, You've Got a Lovely Daughter*, an unashamed US cash-in on the UK pop/ Swinging London phenomenon.

The film soundtrack was done by a strong array of songwriters, producers and session men, including Graham Gouldman, John Paul Jones, Mickie Most and Geoff Stephens. When finally released in September 68, by which point Herman's star was waning, the LP reached number one hundred and eighty two in the US charts. The film, though, recouped its costs and made a decent profit.

In early 69, Klein expanded his empire still further, taking over as manager of The Beatles. His subsequent film ventures included *Blindman*, a spaghetti western starring Ringo Starr, *Concert for Bangladesh* and the Lennon/Yoko Ono avant garde feature *Up Your Legs Forever*.

Released January 1968, 110 minutes, colour
DVD: latest release via Warner Archives, April 2011
SOUNDTRACK: LP released by MGM, September 1968

30 IS A DANGEROUS AGE, CYNTHIA

Joe McGrath directs
Dudley Moore and Suzy Kendall star

Kendall and Moore

An early attempt to make a film star out of Dudley Moore, *30 is a Dangerous Age, Cynthia* was directed by Joe McGrath (who had previously worked with Moore and Peter Cook on both their hit TV series *Not Only… But Also* and the film *Bedazzled*) from a script co-written by Moore and satirist John Wells. Walter Shenson produced, having fulfilled similar duties on *A Hard Day's Night* and *Help!*. Moore co-starred with Suzy Kendall, his wife at the time and on something of a box office roll of her own after her appearance in *To Sir, With Love*. John Bird, first noticed in the TV satire series *That Was the Week That Was* leads the supporting cast, which included Hollywood veteran Eddie Foy Jr. Moore's own career up to this point, which has often been overlooked in the light of his subsequent Hollywood stardom, already included many significant successes in UK stage, revue, jazz, film and TV, stretching back to his involvement with the Royal Court Theatre in the 50s and his contribution to the soundtrack of *Saturday Night and Sunday Morning* in 60.

The plot was suitably daft: a timid piano player – who is struggling to write a musical – can't click with women and is desperate to get married before he reaches 30. Various scrapes ensue. Visually, the film contains many fine pop art set pieces with a nod toward 40s private eye films – not unlike the 71 Albert Finney film *Gumshoe*.

The title music eventually appeared as a Decca single in November 68 and was followed by the soundtrack – which Moore did in a variety of styles – some months later.

Released March 1968, 85 minutes, colour
DVD: video release on Columbia/Tristar in 1997
SOUNDTRACK: Decca LP release as *The Music of Dudley Moore*, 1969. Same LP issued in the US on London as *30 is a Dangerous Age, Cynthia*

UP THE JUNCTION

Peter Collinson directs
Suzy Kendall stars
Manfred Mann do the music

Maureen Lipman and Adrienne Posta down the pub in Up the Junction

A seminal British film of its time, *Up the Junction* was a 'slice of life' working class drama shot in and around Battersea and Clapham. Co-produced by Ned Sherrin, who, like John Bird, had made his reputation with the TV satire show *That Was the Week That Was*, it was directed by Peter Collinson, whose career peaked a couple of years later with *The Italian Job*, and was adapted from a book by Nell Dunn who had also written *Poor Cow* and whose husband, Jeremy Sandford, did the original screenplay for *Cathy Come Home*.

The plot is fairly simple: a comfortably well off girl in Chelsea (Suzy Kendall) moves south of the river to a rough neighbourhood, to live with her boyfriend (Dennis Waterman), and experiences a very different way of life as a result. Waterman, who was from Clapham, might have been born to play the part. Originally noticed as a child actor in the BBC TV series *William*, he would later star in a number of horror and sex films before returning to the small screen, and eventual stardom, in the 70s police thriller series *The Sweeney*. Some critics felt that, even in 68, the sensationalist nature of Dunn's writing, in which 'the working class' is always downtrodden, struggling and miserable, was somewhat obsolete and certainly, within a few years of the film's release, it was hard to see what the fuss had all been about.

The soundtrack was excellent, featuring a fine clutch of songs by Manfred Mann and Mike Hugg, including the title number, which became a major hit for them in the Netherlands, despite flopping elsewhere, as well as Cherry Smash performing the sublime '*Sing Songs of Love*'.

Released March 1968, 119 minutes, colour
DVD: latest release via Paramount Home Entertainment, August 2008
SOUNDTRACK LP: released in UK on Fontana 1968. Reissued on CD 2004

NEROSUBIANCO
(BLACK ON WHITE)

Tinto Brass directs
The Freedom do the music

Anita Sanders

Where Michelangelo Antonioni trod, others soon followed. The international success of *Blow-Up* led to a number of *auteurs* – major and minor, real or would be – hurriedly visiting London to pursue various 'Swinging' projects, most of which contained a marked musical input. One such was fellow Italian Tinto Brass, who shot *Col cuore in gola* in London in early 67 with French mega star Jean-Louis Trintignant and Swedish beauty queen Ewa Aulin – the latter soon to be the centrepiece around which the extravaganza *Candy* revolved. Marketed as a 'pop art murder mystery', it had immense visual style, and a plot so simplistic and unlikely that it resembled a skilfully made live action graphic novel, much in the style of *Modesty Blaise* and *Jeu de Massacre*. With the main characters meeting in a discotheque two minutes into the film, Trintignant seemingly able to wander around odd bits of London with a loaded revolver, and much of the action framed by a sumptuous lounge ballad ('*Love Girl*', sung by Gianni Davoli and arranged/composed by Armando Trovajoli), the end result was certainly entertaining, but barely a commercial success despite being released outside Italy under a variety of different titles: *Heart Beat, I Am What I Am* and *Deadly Sweet*.

A year later, Brass was back with the Dino De Laurentiis produced *Nerosubianco*. Unlike his earlier effort, this had a lightweight cast but clearly imitated *Blow-Up*, with its freewheeling use of London settings and inventive visual trickery. The plot – a stream of consciousness, free association study of the relationship between a white woman and a black man, against a back drop of social and political events – contains, by the standards of the time, explicit sex scenes and features little actual dialogue, being punctuated instead with a series of dreamy voiceovers and sound effects.

A key device used in the story was the creative use of a pop group as a type of Greek chorus ... constantly interpolated into the action and appearing (and performing) in a variety of settings, far more than was the case in other films of the period. For this almost unique role, Brass selected The Freedom, who, when shooting commenced in November 67, had been formed only a few months earlier by the drummer, guitarist and manager of Procol Harum, after they were ousted from that group. What emerged musically, under the supervision of Mike Lease (their keyboards player and formerly a member of The Zephyrs) and Jonathan Weston, their producer, was an album's worth of material that sounded very like a late psychedelic progression from 'A Whiter Shade of Pale' which fits perfectly with the mood and ambience of the film. Premiered at Cannes in May 68, the film was initially banned in Italy, reached the US (as Black on White) in October 69 and appeared – heavily edited – in a few UK sex cinemas, under the title Attraction, in 73 ... by which time, it illustrated an era that had passed.

The soundtrack LP was released on Atlantic, but only in Italy, in 69. What must have seemed an enormous career boost for The Freedom in 67-68, at a time when Procol Harum were faltering slightly after their initial global success, soon fizzled out. After an abortive recording contract with Mercury, the group relaunched themselves in 70 as a rather conventional heavy rock power trio. Today, happily, both Brass's film and The Freedom's soundtrack have been disinterred by the cultural archaeologists and given their due acclaim.

Released May 1968 (Cannes), 77 minutes, colour
DVD: reissued by Cult Epics, September 2009
SOUNDTRACK: LP released on Atlantic in Italy in 1969. CD reissued on Tenth Planet in 1994

The Swinging London Renaissance Man

Was David Hemmings the English Orson Welles? A wunderkind, starting at the top and working his way downwards? First noticed at a mere 13 in Benjamin Britten's impeccably high brow opera *The Turn of the Screw*, he resurfaced at 18 in films – *No Trees In The Street* (juvenile delinquent on a housing estate in east London) and *The Wind of Change* (juvenile delinquent involved in racist goings-on in Portobello Road). From there he moved into a series of vapid pop musicals, often as a band member: *Play It Cool*, *Some People*, *Live It Up!*, *Be My Guest* and – curiously – *Africa Shakes* (filmed in apartheid South Africa with Brian Poole and The Tremeloes and Sharon Tandy).

Blow-Up made him the biggest film star in the world at twenty five (the same age that *Citizen Kane* happened for Welles) and led to a Hollywood offer to act, and sing, in *Camelot*. In LA, he took time out from the shooting schedule to cut an LP with Leon Russell and The Byrds and produced something of a folk rock/psych classic. Unlike most singing actors, he didn't disgrace himself. Back in the UK, he put up the money for Simon Napier-Bell's record label (SNB – distributed by CBS) which released, during its brief lifetime, material by Andy Ellison and Mellow Candle, the latter now highly acclaimed by collectors.

With five consecutive starring roles in UK films between 69 and '71, he could fairly claim to be a box office star and immediately ventured (like Welles) into producing and directing via his company Hemdale. The results were mixed: *Connecting Rooms* (produced – barely seen flop), *Murphy's War* (produced – big success), *Melody* (produced – hit in Japan), *Girl Stroke Boy* (produced – too niche, too advanced, even for 71), *Universal Soldier* (distributed – tanked) and *Running Scared* (wrote and directed – critical success but barely got its money back). By 72, Hemmings was taking smaller roles and doing TV.

Hemdale later co-produced *Tommy* and Hemmings himself directed *Just a Gigolo*, with Bowie and Dietrich, in 78; but, despite these periodic flashes of brilliance, his career, like those of many others during this period, never fulfilled its early potential.

ONLY WHEN I LARF

Basil Dearden directs
David Hemmings stars

The fourth Len Deighton book to be filmed in three years (the others being the Michael Caine spy thrillers *The Ipcress File*, *Funeral in Berlin* and *Billion Dollar Brain*), *Only When I Larf* was directed by Basil Dearden, whose credits in the UK film industry stretched back to the 40s.

An exceptionally entertaining crime caper – a staple plot of Swinging London (and similar) films – it follows a small group of confidence tricksters fleecing their clients in various international locations. The film starred Richard Attenborough and David Hemmings and co-starred Alexandra Stewart who had previously made *Mickey One* with Warren Beatty and who was also seen in a great many Italian, French, Spanish and German productions at this time.

Its musical content was entrusted to Ron Grainer, whose previous work had included themes for the TV series *Dr Who* and *The Prisoner*, soundtracks for *Nothing But the Best* and *To Sir, With Love*, and the production of the classic 60s psych single '*Boy Meets Girl*' by Paper Blitz Tissue. The title song, by Whistling Jack Smith, was released as a single on Deram in June 68, and was the third attempt at a follow up hit to the April 67 worldwide smash '*I was Kaiser Bill's Batman*' (a play on the Notting Hill boutique, 'I Was Lord Kitchener's Valet', that kicked off the fad for second hand Victoriana and surplus military tunics at this time). Smith was actually two different artists: John O'Neill on record (also used by Ennio Morricone to provide the whistling in *The Good, the Bad and the Ugly*) and, in live appearances, Billy Moeller, whose brother was in the pop group Unit 4+2.

Terrence Alexander and David Hemmings

Released May 1968, 104 minutes, colour
DVD: 1980s VHS release – but no availability on CD to date
SOUNDTRACK: None traced

WONDERWALL

Joe Massot directs
George Harrison produces
Jane Birkin stars

Joe Massot came to the attention of the film world in 66 when his fourteen minute short *Reflections on Love* (in which young people and couples, including all four Beatles, talk about relationships) won a prize at the Cannes Film Festival. Emboldened by this success, and after an initial attempt to interest The Bee Gees, he pitched a feature project to George Harrison, hoping that Harrison would want to follow McCartney (*The Family Way*) and Lennon (*How I Won the War*) in a high profile cinematic venture. The result was *Wonderwall*, a surreal, absurdist, psychedelic drama, based on a script by Gérard Brach, a long term collaborator with Roman Polanski, and Guillermo Infante, a Cuban novelist.

The film stars Jack MacGowran, previously seen in *How I Won the War*, as a timid, much put upon, eccentric 'little man' who becomes infatuated by the girl next door – Jane Birkin (playing Penny Lane, and clad in a variety of diaphanous robes and miniscule costumes) in her first starring role. Taking place largely within a series of cramped interiors, the sets were decorated by The Fool, the design collective involved with the launch of the Apple boutique. George Harrison and his Liverpool colleagues, The Remo Four, worked on the soundtrack from November 67 to February 68 and later added to it a heavy dose of Indian music. The film premiered at Cannes in May 68 but was deemed too eclectic for a general release and only limped into UK cinemas in January 69.

The soundtrack fared better. Released in November 68 – and the first LP on the new Apple label – it reached number twenty two in Germany and number forty nine in the US.

Jane, through the Wonderwall

Premiered May 1968, cinema showings from January 1969. 192 minutes, colour
DVD: latest release via Prism Leisure Corporation, October 2005
SOUNDTRACK: LP released via Apple in November 1968. Reissued on CD in 1992

DET VAR EN LØRDAG AFTEN

Daimi stars
Cream do the music

Like most productions shot in Denmark, *Det Var En Lørdag Aften* was made entirely for the domestic market. Written and directed by Erik Balling, it starred Morten Grunwald and Daimi, the latter a well known Danish pop singer (something like a cross between Helen Shapiro and Brenda Lee in UK terms) who appears here in her fifth leading role after moving into films in 66.

Based on a famous nineteenth century (or earlier) ballad about unrequited love, the plot concerns a conventional middle class man making his way across Copenhagen one Saturday evening to visit his girlfriend and getting inadvertently entangled in a long rambling procession of hippies en route to a rock concert. He finds the experience strangely liberating – and has some explaining to do afterwards to his partner. A brief glimpse is thus afforded here of the nascent Danish counter-culture that later came to the fore in the 71 occupation of the Christiania military base by squatters.

The concert consists of The Cream performing from the back of a lorry, and, later in a small impromptu venue, the sequences for this being filmed in four freezing cold days in February 68. An interesting historical curio, most of the sound track came from pianist Bent Fabricius who enjoyed a surprise hit in the US in 62 with *Alley Cat* and whose material turned up subsequently in many films, including *Saturday Night and Sunday Morning* (60) and *The Damned* (63 – Hammer Films and Joseph Losey).

Released 28 June 1968, 84 minutes, colour
DVD: None traced
SOUNDTRACK: No release

WORK IS A FOUR LETTER WORD

Peter Hall directs
David Warner and Cilla Black star

Directed by Peter Hall and essentially a film project for the Royal Shakespeare Company, this has one of the more curious plots found in a UK 60s feature. Based on the Henry Livings absurdist farce *Eh?* (which had been a major Broadway hit for a pre-*Graduate* Dustin Hoffman), the story is about a man who cannot raise any enthusiasm to work in a 'proper' nine to five job and would sooner spend his time growing hallucinogenic mushrooms. Eventually, he gets a job working in a power station – for a distant, uninterested, bureaucratic employer – but uses this as an excuse to indulge his hobby: with disastrous consequences for the inhabitants of the town he lives in.

The film starred David Warner, who had been seen in a not dissimilar eccentric leading role in *Morgan – A Suitable Case for Treatment*, and, for reasons not clear, Cilla Black, in her only significant acting part. (Perhaps, given that 67-68 were the years that John Lennon appeared in *How I Won The War*, George Harrison did *Wonderwall* and the Fab Four produced their cartoon epic *Yellow Submarine*, it seemed only natural in some quarters that a Merseybeat fellow traveller should also do something suitably leftfield).

Black also sang the theme title, which was produced by George Martin, and duly released as the b-side to her single 'Where is Tomorrow?' in June 68. (Bizarrely, it was covered by The Smiths in 87). The soundtrack also contains material composed for the film by Delia Derbyshire of the BBC Radiophonic Workshop, and is thus a rare example of her work in this medium.

Cilla Black in the studio with producer George Martin

Released June 1968, 93 minutes, colour
DVD: Currently available via The Video Beat
SOUNDTRACK: No release

YELLOW SUBMARINE

George Dunning directs
Erich Segal does the script

The Beatles in Pepperland

Something of an indulgent apogee in the career of The Beatles, *Yellow Submarine* was the first British cartoon feature to be released since *Animal Farm* (54). It was directed by George Dunning, a Canadian animator who had previously produced the excellent opening title sequence for the Inspector Clouseau farce *A Shot in the Dark*, before enjoying a major success in 65-67 with the hugely popular US cartoon series *The Beatles*.

On *Yellow Submarine*, he was assisted by Al Brodax, previously responsible for the *Popeye the Sailor Man* series, Jack Mendelsohn, who later graduated to *Teenage Mutant Hero Turtles*, and Erich Segal, who wrote the surrealist/fantasy script. This was heavily based around Beatles songs and had some uncredited help from Roger McGough. The ending of the film – stressing the overwhelming importance of love – prefigures Segal's massive 70 feature movie hit *Love Story*. Visually brilliant and including much inventive (and expensive) imagery, the voices for the film's characters were provided by, among others, Dick Emery and Lance Percival.

The Beatles recorded only two new songs for the soundtrack, relying instead, as they had in *Magical Mystery Tour*, on material left over from '*Sgt. Pepper*', the title song (a hit in 66) and a hefty instrumental contribution from the George Martin Orchestra. Released as an LP in January 69, it reached number three in the UK charts and number two in the US.

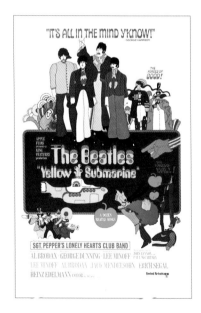

Released 17 July 1968, 90 minutes, colour
DVD: Latest reissue via Apple Corps, May 2012
SOUNDTRACK: LP released on Apple, January 1969

SETTE VOLTE SETTE
(SEVEN TIMES SEVEN)

Michele Lupo directs
The Casuals do the music

A rarely seen star vehicle for Gastone Moschin, who also wrote the script, *Sette volte Sette* was directed by Michele Lupo and featured a cast more normally seen in classical epics and spaghetti westerns (Lionel Stander, Raimondo Vianello and Gordon Mitchell) bulked out here, because of the 'Swinging London' locations, with some reliable British supporting faces, including Terry-Thomas.

The plot would be strangely familiar to contemporary UK cineastes: a robbery (in this case of the Royal Mint) is planned by inmates of a jail; the robbery takes place in a crowded city whilst the population are distracted in this case by the FA Cup final and the police hampered in their attempts to pursue the perpetrators; the crooks get away in an iconic vehicle (in this case, a red double-decker bus). The basic similarities to *The Italian Job*, filmed some while later, are clear – so much so that *Sette volte Sette* might be regarded as the Italian version of *The Italian Job*. Yet another variant, or at least another example at this time of the vogue for heist movies with improbable plots, would be the French/Italian *Le Cerveau/ The Brain* in which a criminal mastermind (David Niven) plans the theft of secret NATO funds as they are shipped across Europe. This includes an obligatory Carnaby Street sequence and has US group The American Breed doing the main theme.

Moschin later returned to the UK to star in the superior Italian giallo thriller *The Weekend Murders* (1970). The soundtrack was scored by the legendary Armando Trovajoli and features The Casuals, a major draw in Italy and the UK at this point, performing the title song.

Released 1968, 92 minutes (105 minutes in Italian and Greek versions), colour
DVD: Released in Japan in 1999 on King.
SOUNDTRACK LP: Released on Jolly Records in Italy in 1969. CD reissue in Japan in 2000 on Seven Seas

BABY LOVE

Michael Klinger produces
Katch-22 do the music

The career of *Baby Love* producer Michael Klinger encapsulates much of the puzzling journey that the UK film industry went on in the 60s and 70s: moments of undeniable class (*Cul-de-Sac* and *Get Carter*) spiralling down to a conclusion with the *Confessions* series. *Baby Love* occupies a slot midway between these extremes.

Supposedly a starring vehicle for Diana Dors (who appears in it for barely five minutes), with a plot about the sexual adventures of a 15-year-old girl (Linda Hayden, later a stalwart of Hammer horrors), it proved to be the prototype for a number of similar ventures in the following years, all of which explored, exploited or denounced matters to do with the age of consent, the permissive society, (very) young girls going off with middle aged men and the danger of exposing the youth of the day to drugs and loud music etc. Troy Dante, a now forgotten recording artist of the time, appears in an acting role in the cast – a position presumably owed to his being managed by Diana Dors.

The soundtrack was written and performed by the UK psych group Katch-22, also seen in action in an extended discotheque sequence.

Released September 1968, 93 minutes, colour
DVD: Video released by Polygram in August 1994
SOUNDTRACK: No release

THE COMMITTEE

Paul Jones stars
Pink Floyd do the music

Produced and written by Max Steuer, a lecturer at the London School of Economics (where much of the film was shot, to keep down costs), *The Committee* is a serious, talkative, supporting feature about how society in the future might choose to regulate those deemed liable to commit anti-social or criminal behaviour.

Syd Barrett.

Directed by Peter Sykes, who had previously worked on the anti-Vietnam war documentary *Tell Me Lies*, the film, rather like *Separation*, attempts to put dramatic clothing on the theories of RD Laing about how madness is defined, by whom, and how society should react to its manifestations. Filming took place in the autumn and winter of 67, with a cast headed by Paul Jones, appearing here in his second starring role after *Privilege*. Steuer, on the basis of his friendship with Peter Jenner (at that stage still manager of Pink Floyd, and a colleague of his at the LSE), initially approached Syd Barrett to do the soundtrack being unaware, when he did so, that Barrett was being increasingly marginalised within Pink Floyd. After a single day's recording in January 68, Barrett was dropped abruptly (on grounds of cost – the film had an almost zero budget) and replaced by the rest of Pink Floyd, who quickly stepped in and produced an LP's worth of instrumental material that has yet to be properly released in any format. The remainder of the score was provided by The Crazy World of Arthur Brown, who perform their single 'Nightmare' in a party sequence, and provide a moody keyboards instrumental passage.

Some interest still attends Barrett's slender and abortive contribution, now seemingly lost and recorded with an unknown bass player and drummer. When interviewed in 2012, Steuer was able only to recollect that it was 'jazzy, with a groove'.

Released September 1968, 58 minutes, black and white
DVD: Released by Electric in July 2005
SOUNDTRACK: No formal release

THE BLISS OF MRS BLOSSOM

Joe McGrath directs
Richard Attenborough stars

An overblown and extravagant film, which given it was directed by Joe McGrath whose other work included *Casino Royale*, *The Magic Christian* and the TV series *Not Only... But Also* was hardly surprising, this was produced by Paramount and has a coarse, farcical, storyline not unlike the work of Joe Orton.

With production design by Assheton Gorton, whose credits also included *The Knack*, *Blow-Up*, *Wonderwall*, *The Bed-Sitting Room* and *Get Carter*, the film is decked out with archetypal swinging 60s trappings – huge pop art sets, the very latest trends in fashion, furniture, clothing, music and cars etc. McGrath co-wrote the absurdist script with Dennis Norden about a brassiere manufacturer (Richard Attenborough) who secretly yearns to be an orchestra conductor, whilst his neglected wife, Shirley MacLaine, keeps her lover in the attic. Bruce Lacey, Tony Gray and Douglas Gray appear in minor supporting roles. Known as The Alberts (or even The Massed Alberts, as in the massed bands of the Grenadier Guards etc), they had been active since the 50s satirising the public school/officer class and were early exponents of the craze for Victoriana that later became emblematic of the *Sgt. Pepper* period. A bit too old and early to catch the Swinging London bandwagon, they worked with Spike Milligan, had a big success with the revue *An Evening of British Rubbish* (62-63) and landed a recording deal with EMI/Parlophone, where George Martin produced them. Lacey, in particular, had a long career within UK counter-culture from the satire boom of the early 60s through poetry readings at the Albert Hall to supporting Pink Floyd – with his bubble machine – at a festival in Brighton in 67. He appeared in both *Help!* and *Smashing Time* and, in 65, built and exhibited on the avant-garde art scene an automated female robot – Rosa Bosom – whose name suggests a connection of sorts with this film.

The soundtrack includes material by The New Vaudeville Band and The Spectrum, the latter a British group intended by RCA Records to replicate the global success of US Beatles copyists The Monkees.

Released September 1968, 93 minutes, colour
DVD: Released by Paramount In 1992
SOUNDTRACK: LP released on RCA Victor in 1968

BETTER A WIDOW
(MEGLIO VEDOVA)

Duccio Tessari directs
Virna Lisi and Peter McEnery star

Following in the footsteps of Antonioni and Tinto Brass, Duccio Tessari filmed part of his romantic mafia comedy/crime caper *Better a Widow/Meglio vedova* in London in late 67 and early 68. Made exclusively for the French and Italian domestic markets, it followed his work on the spaghetti western *A Pistol for Ringo* (65) and the spy satire *Kiss Kiss Bang Bang* (66).

Starring Virna Lisi and Peter McEnery, the plot concerns an English engineer, working in the south of Italy, who falls for the daughter of a wealthy man and finds, as a result, that he has to overcome the machinations of the local mafia. Jean Servais and Gabriele Ferzetti co-star, Ferzetti being quite a figure at this time with major roles in *Once Upon a Time in the West*, *Machine Gun McCain* and *On Her Majesty's Secret Service*.

A brief segment was filmed in Hyde Park and shows the stars dancing to The Mike Stuart Span who, a few months after the appearance of the film, relaunched themselves as the progressive group Leviathan. The soundtrack was otherwise undertaken by veteran Carlo Rustichelli.

Virna Lisi

Released 9 October 1968, 105 minutes, colour
DVD: No release
SOUNDTRACK: No UK or US release

THE GIRL ON A MOTORCYCLE

Jack Cardiff directs
Marianne Faithfull and Alain Delon star

The first film produced by Radio Caroline entrepreneur Ronan O'Rahilly, *The Girl on a Motorcycle* was directed by Jack Cardiff and shot on location in Europe, in the first six months of 68.

Based on a novel by the French surrealist writer André Pieyre de Mandiargues, about a young woman who travels, by motorbike, between her husband and lover, it starred Marianne Faithfull and Alain Delon. The job of making the dialogue comprehensible to modern audiences fell to Gillian Freeman, whose previous work had included the book and screenplay for *The Leather Boys* (63) which starred Rita Tushingham and explored a gay relationship between two young working class men. O'Rahilly's film was a modest success on the art house circuit despite being regarded with scorn by some reviewers, one of whom called it 'sub porn clap trap', possibly a not unfair description given that de Mandiargues personally owned a substantial collection of pornographic material and had written the introduction to the 54 bondage/sado-masochism novel *The Story of O* (a film of which was later due to appear in 73-74 produced by Allen Klein, with Alejandro Jodorowsky directing… it eventually got made by Just Jaeckin as his follow up to *Emmanuelle*).

Marianne Faithfull

In the US, O'Rahilly's film was released as *Naked Under Leather*, reflecting a view (then) that wearing leather and little else was deeply erotic. The soundtrack was produced by Les Reed, the former pianist in The John Barry Seven, who, like Barry, had moved into film.

Released October 1968, 91 minutes, colour
DVD: Released on Kino Lorber, April 2011
SOUNDTRACK: LP released on Polydor 1968. Reissued on RPM as LP and CD 1996

OTLEY

Dick Clement and Ian La Frenais direct
Romy Schneider and Tom Courtenay star

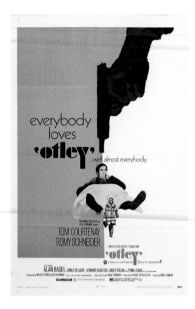

When Romy Schneider, one of the great international film actresses of the 60s with starring roles in films by Ophuls, Visconti and Welles, came to London to film *Otley*, she made the point of saying it was 'because it was made by young talented people'. This was certainly the case with Dick Clement (31) and Ian La Frenais (32), who wrote and directed and whose reputation had by then been secured by the massively successful TV series *The Likely Lads* and their debut feature film *The Jokers*. She could also have been referring to her co-star Tom Courtenay (31) then at the pinnacle of his box office appeal and to Martin Waddell (27), the author of the comedy thriller the film was based on. Waddell had briefly been a professional footballer some years earlier (with Fulham) and this experience, as a young working class man adrift in a big city, seems to have seeped into the plot, where a similar figure has various misadventures whilst at large around London.

Essentially an espionage comedy/drama with Bond trappings, the action takes place in the heavily circumscribed set of London locations (Notting Hill Gate, a houseboat on the Thames at Chelsea, the Bunny Club etc) so beloved by UK film makers at this time. Courtenay's performance as a useless layabout, who is mistakenly believed to be a secret agent, is especially entertaining. The supporting cast, led by Alan Badel and James Villiers, is outstanding.

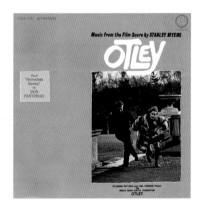

The pop sensibilities are stamped on the film from the opening sequence, where Courtenay meanders along Portobello Road to the title theme music: Don Partridge singing '*Homeless Bones*', duly released as the b-side to his May 69 single '*Colour My World*'. Elsewhere, The Herd can be spotted making a split second appearance at a Buckingham Palace investiture scene. *Otley* was a popular box office success in the UK and was also regarded by critics as one of the better quality British releases of the year. Waddell wrote several sequels, none of which seemed to interest either film or TV people. He later scored a huge success with the 88 children's book '*Can't You Sleep Little Bear?*'.

Released October 1968,
91 minutes, colour
**DVD: Released by Sony Pictures,
August 2010**
SOUNDTRACK LP/CD:
Originally released on RCA in 1969.
No subsequent CD reissue

SYMPATHY FOR THE DEVIL
(ONE PLUS ONE)

Jean-Luc Godard directs
The Rolling Stones star

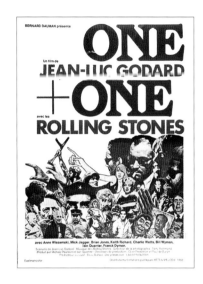

A fiercely political, agit-prop, art house documentary/drama, directed by Jean-Luc Godard, *Sympathy for the Devil* is his study of the counter-culture of the time and features a semi-random collage of The Rolling Stones rehearsing and recording the title song, intercut with various shots of the Black Panthers, feminists and far right activists and other assorted figures.

The main acting roles are taken by Anne Wiazemsky (Godard's wife and a regular in European art films at this time) and Iain Quarrier, who co-produced the project. Quarrier later fell out badly with Godard after taking it on himself to alter the film's closing sequences and is now an archetypal 'lost' figure of the era. His career would never surpass the work credited to him in a few years in the late 60s: appearing in *Separation* and *Wonderwall*, producing the still unreleased *Last of The Long-Haired Boys*, a collaborator with Roman Polanski and Sharon Tate (by whose death he was devastated) and attached – in some way – as 'creative associate' to the quintessential US road movie *Vanishing Point*.

Godard meets The Rolling Stones

Plagued by endless production problems, the film remained a staple of late night cinema club and university audiences for many years, after its belated appearance.

Released December 1968, 100 minutes, colour
DVD: Released on Fabulous Films, 2005
SOUNDTRACK: No formal release

THE ROLLING STONES ROCK AND ROLL CIRCUS

Michael Lindsay-Hogg directs
The Rolling Stones star

Mick Jagger at the circus

A TV special, intended to do for The Rolling Stones what it was felt *Magical Mystery Tour* had done for The Beatles, *Rock and Roll Circus* was filmed in the final months of 68 – thus offering the last footage of Brian Jones with the group – by Michael Lindsay-Hogg, whose previous credits included various promotional films for both The Beatles and The Rolling Stones as well as a stint on *Ready Steady Go!*.

Set in a large marquee and interspersed with shots of performing acrobats etc, the film contains high quality musical performances from The Who, Jethro Tull and Taj Mahal, an impromptu jam session with John Lennon, Mitch Mitchell and Eric Clapton and appearances by both Marianne Faithfull and Yoko Ono. The Rolling Stones' own contribution, which in retrospect seems fine, was felt by them at the time to be less than successful: so much so that the release/broadcast of the material was abandoned and the completed work not subsequently seen for twenty eight years.

Michael Lindsay-Hogg, whom film buffs may note was later found to be the love child of Orson Welles, went on to direct *Let It Be*.

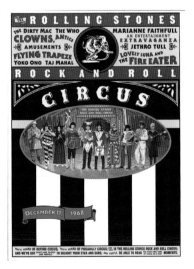

Released 1996 (filmed December 1968), 65 minutes, colour
DVD: Released 2004
SOUNDTRACK: LP released on ABKCO, October 1996

THE TOUCHABLES

Robert Freeman directs
Judy Huxtable stars

The second film to be funded from the profits made by *The Sound of Music*, *The Touchables* was directed by Robert Freeman, who had previously done the title sequences for *A Hard Day's Night*, *The Knack* and *Help!* The script was a collaborative effort from Donald Cammell, David Cammell (his brother) and Ian La Frenais, which, with its kinky sex, suggestion of the occult and central plot device of the hero being pursued by a gang of gay heavies, clearly prefigures *Performance*.

Set at some point in the near future, it centres on a group of young women played by Judy Huxtable, also seen in *Scream and Scream Again*, Esther Anderson, a former Miss Jamaica and Top of the Pops dancer, Marilyn Rickard and Kathy Simmonds. Decked out in a variety of riotous and fashionable garb they kidnap a pop star and take him to the inflatable plastic bubble where they live (inflatable plastic homes being commonly thought in 68 to be the most likely type of housing in the near future) and use him as a sex slave. In an indication of the anything is possible and anything might sell attitude of the time, the male lead is played by David Anthony, like Freeman a photographer, but neither an actor nor a pop star. He did, though, do the cover photographs for the 69 '*Deep Purple*' LP.

Unlike its contemporary *Joanna*, *The Touchables* was not a commercial success and disappeared from view very quickly. The film soundtrack includes material by Wynder K Frog and Ferris Wheel whilst Nirvana released the main theme *All of Us (The Touchables)* as a single in late 68, without success. Heard in the background, and once again proving their ability to crop up in as many films as possible at this time, are The Pink Floyd, playing part of '*Interstellar Overdrive*'.

Marilyn Rickard

Released November 1968, 97 minutes, colour
DVD: None released to date.
SOUNDTRACK: LP released on EMI Stateside in 1969

JOANNA

Mike Sarne directs
Geneviève Waite and Donald Sutherland star

The career of Mike Sarne is one of the great cautionary tales of the 60s. Originally an actor-singer and managed, like John Leyton, by Robert Stigwood, he burst on the scene in 62-63 with four hit singles (including a number one, *Come Outside*) delivered in the deadpan cockney layabout style of Anthony Newley… which was odd given that he was from a family of Czech refugees and had a Bachelor of Arts degree in Russian. Like most pop stars, he went straight into films but, unlike most, managed to avoid absolute junk. He was a delinquent in the east end of London with Rita Tushingham in *A Place to Go* (63) and a David Hemmings type fashion photographer in *Two Weeks in September* (67), alongside Brigitte Bardot, with whom he had an affair. Not long after this he pitched an idea to Twentieth Century Fox: a female version of *Alfie* shot in London in the style of *La Dolce Vita*. Awash with money after the blockbusting success of *The Sound of Music*, the highest grossing film in history at that point, Fox agreed and advanced him $1,000,000/£350,000 to make *Joanna*. (Approximately £8m today: they also commissioned Robert Freeman, The Beatles photographer, to make *The Touchables* at the same time, for the same budget. It's ironic that the wholesome *Sound of Music* should have paid for such permissive excesses and another illustration of how much Swinging London relied on Hollywood funding).

Sarne, twenty seven, had never directed or written a feature before. His film was designed by Michael Wield in the style of a series of fashion magazine photo shoots (today we would say music videos) with sumptuous photography from Walter Lassally. (Both Wield and Lassally worked on *Twinky* eighteen months later). The plot centres on a teenage girl arriving in London to go to art school and sleeping around; with its various diversions – including a scene of an elephant being ridden down Bond Street – there are similarities to the Terry Southern extravaganza *Candy*: both films have non-acting heroines – Geneviève Waite, a South African model in *Joanna* and Ewa Aulin, a Swedish beauty queen in *Candy*; both heroines stumble through a range of sexual encounters with the opposite sex and both play characters who are wide-eyed innocents.

Given that both were filmed at the same time, one wonders if Twentieth Century Fox backed *Joanna* to cash in on the same market as *Candy*. Shot mainly in London, with additional sequences in Morocco (emerging as a hippy holiday destination at this point), Sarne's film co-starred Donald Sutherland and Calvin Lockhart, and was successful on release, unlike *The Touchables*, which quickly disappeared from view. Sarne, Waite, Lockhart and Sutherland duly followed the money trail back to Hollywood with mixed results. Waite married John Phillips (of The Mamas and The Papas) and spent years with him writing and trying, unsuccessfully, to get funding for a rock musical film of the moon landings starring Elvis Presley. Lockhart appeared in a couple of the better 'blaxploitation' films of the early 70s (*Halls of Anger* and *Cotton Comes to Harlem*), and Sutherland went straight to *MASH* and international stardom. Sarne was given carte blanche by Twentieth Century Fox and directed *Myra Breckenridge* (70). After this failed, completely, he was disowned by Hollywood and became one of many associated with Swinging London and the 60s generally who disappeared suddenly from public view.

Glenna Forster-Jones

The Scott Walker hit '*Joanna*' is not included on the soundtrack, although its chart run six months prior probably helped sell the film. The score was done by Rod McKuen, a San Francisco beat poet who relocated to France in the 60s and worked with Serge Gainsbourg and Jacques Brel. (Brel was a favourite composer of Walker's too). McKuen composed an album of material, mostly in the same folk-pop style of Georgy Girl. It was one of three major soundtracks he did at this time, the others being *The Prime of Miss Jean Brodie* and *Me, Nathalie*.

Released December 1968, 108 minutes, colour
DVD: Reissued by BFI Video 2011
SOUNDTRACK: Released on EMI Stateside in 1968

THE VIRGIN SOLDIERS

John Dexter directs
Hywel Bennett and Lynn Redgrave star

A massive box office hit in the UK, *The Virgin Soldiers* successfully merged a number of genres: the traditional British war film, the disenchantment of the earlier 'kitchen sink' dramas and the 'swinging' youth movie. Based on a bestselling memoir by Leslie Thomas, whose book of the same title appeared in 66, the plot concerns the tribulations of a group of National Servicemen in Malaya in the 50s.

David Bowie on National Service

Scripted by John McGrath (whose previous credits included the Harry Palmer/Michael Caine thriller *Billion Dollar Brain*) and John Hopkins (who had worked on *Thunderball*), the film was directed by John Dexter, one of the great UK theatrical figures of the time, whose successes included *The Royal Hunt of the Sun* and Olivier's *Othello* (both 64). In what was clearly a pitch for the pop market, the lead roles were played by Lynn Redgrave and Hywel Bennett, rather than any of the slightly older actors more typically seen in works of this type. Among the conscripts can be found David Bowie – in transit at this point from his *faux* Anthony Newley incarnation to his initial success with 'Space Oddity'– glimpsed (and heard) in a miniscule supporting role, Gregory Phillips, a one time recording artist on Pye and Immediate, and a very young Wayne Sleep, playing a gay soldier.

The film opens with a brilliant animated title sequence, plotting the history and heroism of the British Army down the centuries, to the accompaniment of The Kinks' instrumental track 'The Ballad of the Virgin Soldiers'. Inexplicably, it was never commercially released but would have been perfectly at home on their 69 LP 'Arthur (Or the Decline and Fall of the British Empire)'. The film tanked in the US. Whilst their nation was mired in Vietnam, American audiences had little interest in being reminded that the British, too, had been engaged in conflict in South East Asia throughout the 50s and 60s and its very English deadpan and anti-heroic sense of humour did not commend it either. A sequel, *Stand Up Virgin Soldiers*, appeared in 77, with an almost completely different cast, to less box office success.

Released 1969, 96 minutes, colour
DVD: Released by UCA, January 2005
SOUNDTRACK LP/CD:
Original soundtrack LP issued 1969.
No subsequent release

THE GURU

James Ivory directs
Michael York and Rita Tushingham star

The second film from the independent team
of Ismail Merchant and James Ivory to make a
significant impact in the West (the first being
Shakespeare Wallah), *The Guru* was scripted
by their long-standing collaborator Ruth
Prawer Jhabvala and backed financially by
Twentieth Century Fox.

Pleasant to look at and including much
travelogue style footage of India, it reflects
the growing traffic and interaction between
the counter-culture of the West and the sub-
continent in the 60s, a phenomenon largely
started when The Beatles and their entourage
met the Maharishi in 67, blossoming within a few
years into the well trodden hippy trail to Goa, Kabul
and many other points east. A moderate success when
released, *The Guru* stars Rita Tushingham and Michael York,
with York playing a cockney pop star who travels to India to learn
the sitar - as had George Harrison and several others only a little while
previously.

Michael York

In the film York sings (*Tom's Boat Song*) and his contribution is included
on the soundtrack, the music for which was composed by Ustad Vilayat
Khan – one of many Indian sitar players and traditional musicians briefly
in vogue at this time.

Released February 1969, 112 minutes, colour
DVD: No current release
SOUNDTRACK LP: Released on RCA, 1969

WHAT'S GOOD
FOR THE GOOSE

Norman Wisdom stars
The Pretty Things do the music

An enormous box office draw in UK domestic films in the 50s and 60s, Norman Wisdom belatedly tried to update his image towards the end of the decade, ditching his character as the gormless, good-hearted and ultimately triumphant Norman Pitkin in favour of very slightly more elaborate but equally put upon figures. After a supporting role in the US feature *The Night They Raided Minsky's* (68), he returned to the UK to make *What's Good for the Goose* – a film he co-produced and co-wrote with Menahem Golan, a major figure in Israeli cinema who would go on to have a lengthy career producing and directing a number of successful, but often critically panned, melodramas.

The plot concerns a mild mannered bank clerk (Wisdom) who has a midlife crisis, freaks out and joins a group of hippies. Sally Geeson (sister of Judy) co-stars, briefly appearing topless in a scene with Wisdom, the footage of which was cut from the UK release. Much of the filming took place in and around Southport and Merseyside – both locations convenient for Wisdom, who resided on the Isle of Man.

The soundtrack contains five songs by The Pretty Things (including the excellent *Alexandra* and *Eagle's Son*) who also appear in the film as The Electric Banana, the pseudonym they used when composing incidental film music for the De Wolfe soundtrack library in the 60s and 70s with Reg Tilsley, who, like them, also contributes to the score here. Other material was provided by Alan Blaikley and Ken Howard, massively successful songwriters at this time with a string of hit compositions for The Herd, Lulu and Dave Dee, Dozy, Beaky, Mick and Tich.

Wisdom and Geeson

Released March 1969, 105 minutes (cut to 98 minutes in the UK), colour
DVD: Available via Odeon Entertainment
SOUNDTRACK LP: None released. The Electric Banana tracks appeared on '*Even More Electric Banana*' (1969)

The Tilsley Connection

If Pete Frame, genealogist in chief of the tangled web of band line-ups, ever does a rock family tree of film music composers, one branch would lead from John Barry to Les Reed to Reg Tilsley; and thence from Tilsley to The Pretty Things, one of the greatest – and most consistently underrated – of UK pop and rock acts in the 60s. So who was Reg Tilsley?

Like Barry and Reed, he emerged from the world of big band orchestras, dance halls, radio shows and anonymous backing duties, rising to a position as a producer and arranger at Fontana records. Here he was drafted in to do the orchestral scoring on The Pretty Things LP *'Emotions'*, released in April 67 when their initial commercial success was slipping away. Like Les Reed, Tilsley also worked frequently for De Wolfe Music, recording library music in a wide variety of styles for use in film and TV. He persuaded The Pretty Things that as much of their output was not selling well they too could supplement their income by doing this.

Whilst Tilsley arranged the music for *The Mini-Affair* (and later produced the big pop hit by Dave Dee, Dozy, Beaky, Mick and Tich, *'Last Night in Soho'*), The Pretty Things took up his offer and, adopting the Andy Warhol/ Donovan influenced pseudonym of The Electric Banana, cut two LPs for De Wolfe in 67 whilst signed to EMI and working on their groundbreaking rock opera *'SF Sorrow'*.

The debut (made with the Reg Tilsley Orchestra) contained the track *'Cause I'm a Man'* that cropped up as late as 78 in *Dawn of the Dead*. The second has *'Grey Skies'*, used in *The Haunted House of Horror* and the third (*'Even More Electric Banana'*) has the material used in the film *What's Good for the Goose*, in which the group appeared in their pomp. For the next fifteen years, bits and pieces of Electric Banana turned up on the soundtracks of UK features, sex films, documentaries, so much so that one wonders if the group made as much money from this as they did from their other 'legit' work.

IF IT'S TUESDAY, THIS MUST BE BELGIUM

Ian McShane stars
Donovan does the music

Aimed squarely at the US market, *If It's Tuesday, This Must Be Belgium* was produced by David Wolper and directed by Mel Stuart – a team whose substantial list of credits includes many documentaries, notably *Wattstax* (73).

Concerning a group of US tourists on a coaching holiday in Europe, it was filmed extensively on location, with London sequences containing the now obligatory shots of Carnaby Street. Ian McShane, in *Alfie* mode as a womanising Brit, plays the leading role as the tour guide. Donovan appears singing *'Lord of the Reedy River'* (a track that turned up on his 71 LP *'HMS Donovan'*) in a youth hostel. Hopscotch, an underrated late period UK psychedelic group, and previously house band at The Scotch of St James, can be heard on the soundtrack LP. The film was hugely successful: the twenty fifth top grossing US film of 69 and was number one at the box office for four consecutive weeks between *Goodbye Columbus* and *Midnight Cowboy*. Donovan also wrote the main theme, performed here by JP Rags, a pseudonym for an obscure west coast record producer Doug Cox, whose sole album boasted sleeve notes by Nilsson, no less.

A fine piece of folk-rock with a morning-after-the-party feel, the title song seems to signal the end of an era – which, given how quickly Rags and Hopscotch were forgotten and this type of film passed into history, proved to be accurate.

Released April 1969, 99 minutes, colour
DVD: Released on MGM Home Video, May 2008
SOUNDTRACK LP: Released on United Artists 1969

THE RECKONING

Jack Gold directs
Nicol Williamson stars

A very well made and observed dose of social realism, *The Reckoning* shows the other side of the Swinging Sixties: working class life in the North of England. Directed by Jack Gold from a script by John McGrath (whose excellent run of film work at this time included *Billion Dollar Brain*, *The Bofors Gun* and *The Virgin Soldiers*), the plot is about a successful businessman in London returning to Liverpool to sort out some personal matters after a death in the family. The dismal setting – Liverpool looks truly miserable in 68 – is so pronounced that it seems little wonder so many successful Merseybeat acts quit the city a few years earlier.

Preceding the much better known – and successful – *Get Carter* by eighteen months, *The Reckoning* stars Nicol Williamson (giving a full-on bullish performance) and Tom Kempinski, previously seen in *The Committee*. Ann Bell, seen in a supporting role in *To Sir, With Love*, co-stars.

The film includes an appearance, in a club scene, by The Spectrum. The soundtrack was composed by Malcolm Arnold and proved to be his last piece of film work, though not his last involvement with pop and rock: he conducted the Royal Philharmonic Orchestra on their 70 LP outing with Deep Purple, *'Concerto for Group and Orchestra'*.

Nicol Williamson and Rachel Roberts

Released 1969, 111 minutes, colour
DVD: No official release
SOUNDTRACK LP: None released

SUPERSHOW

John Crome directs
Led Zeppelin are the star act

Page and Plant in full swing

After *Monterey Pop* the rock concert film was big business in US drive-ins, campuses and ballrooms and any UK band trying to break that market would have been well advised to produce some footage of themselves for distribution on the other side of the pond. Thus arose *Supershow*, a mixture of live performance, extended rehearsal and jamming. Managing the blistering volume many bands now played at meant that the action was filmed in front of an invited audience in an enormous disused linoleum factory in Staines, in early 69, with the nearest housing about a half mile distant. Produced by Tom Parkinson – who later wrote the screenplays for two satanic horror films, *Crucible of Terror* and *Disciple of Death*, both starring Radio One DJ Mike Raven – it was directed by experienced film editor John Crome and has similarities to *The Rolling Stones Rock and Roll Circus*.

The assorted talents of Led Zeppelin, Colosseum, The Misunderstood, Duster Bennett, The Modern Jazz Quartet, Eric Clapton, Jack Bruce, Buddy Miles, Buddy Guy, Roland Kirk and Stephen Stills are on display. Somewhat ramshackle in parts, and filmed in the cinema verité style of the time, it had an extraordinarily generous budget of £100,000: £7.25m in 2014 money.

The film contains eighteen separate pieces of music but, for reasons that are not clear, no soundtrack LP was ever issued.

Released November 1969, 70 minutes, colour
DVD: Released June 2008 via Eagle Rock Entertainment Limited
SOUNDTRACK LP: No release.

THE HAUNTED HOUSE OF HORROR

Michael Armstrong directs
Frankie Avalon and Mark Wynter star

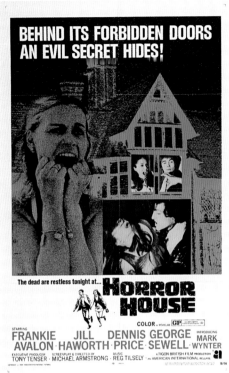

From the mid 50s onwards, American Independent Pictures produced a huge number of cheap dramas, thrillers, comedies and musicals for the US teenage market. With *Haunted House of Horror*, they ventured into the UK, retaining a star familiar to US audiences (Frankie Avalon) and a hackneyed plot (teenagers get stuck in a gloomy old house and terrible things start happening), still serving as the basis of supernatural thrillers and slasher films forty years later.

The film was directed and written by Michael Armstrong, only twenty five years old at the time, who had previously made the 67 short *The Image*, with David Bowie. Armstrong had wanted Bowie for this film in a supporting role but was overruled by AIP. Supporting roles are played by Jill Haworth, the reliable Dennis Price and Mark Wynter, the latter a significant UK pop star in the pre-Beatle period.

The soundtrack was arranged and conducted by Reg Tilsley (who also did *The Mini-Affair* and *What's Good for the Goose*) and featured, like *What's Good for the Goose*, a Pretty Things/Electric Banana song – '*Grey Skies*'.

Released July 1969, 92 minutes, colour
DVD: Released November 2011, via Odeon Entertainment
SOUNDTRACK LP: None released

MORE

Barbet Schroeder directs
Pink Floyd do the music

The directorial debut of Barbet Schroeder, who had previously produced *La Collectionneuse*, *More* was a modestly budgeted feature, partly filmed in Ibiza. The storyline, a counter-culture version of the standard road-to-ruin-via-drug plot, is about a German student who hitchhikes across Europe, meets an American girl and becomes a heroin addict, with predictably unfortunate consequences.

Mimsy Farmer and Klaus Grunberg in Ibiza

The film starred Mimsy Farmer (previously seen in a number of low budget US youth films, including *Riot on Sunset Strip*) and Klaus Grunberg, and was popular at the time, and for some years after, with student audiences, private cinemas and art houses generally.

Schroeder commissioned an entire soundtrack from Pink Floyd, their second such undertaking after *The Committee*. Recorded in March 69, it features the outstanding opening track *'Cirrus Minor'* and was released as an LP (their first with no contribution at all from Syd Barrett) in July 69, reaching number nine in UK, number two in France and an encouraging number one hundred and fifty three in the US, excellent for a contemporary soundtrack LP but representing something of a falling away (in the UK) from the sales their first two albums enjoyed.

Released August 1969, 117 minutes, colour
DVD: Released by BFI Video, September 2011
SOUNDTRACK LP: Released by Pink Floyd on EMI/Columbia in July 1969

PAROXISMUS
(VENUS IN FURS)

Jesus Franco directs
Manfred Mann does the music

Also known as *Venus in Furs*, but with few similarities to Masoch's legendary work of the same name, Paroxismus was written and directed by Jesus Franco, whose credits include a vast number of sex/exploitation works. The plot, about an American jazz musician letting his hair down and his creative juices flow whilst resident abroad – in this instance in Istanbul – stars James Darren, as the central character who finds the body of a dead woman on a beach. The victim subsequently (and ludicrously) re-appears in the film, to take revenge on the gang of sadists responsible for her death.

Darren was a US pop star who also had a substantial acting career, notably in surfing dramas such as *Gidget* and *For Those Who Think Young*. The main supporting roles were played by Barbara McNair, a Tamla Motown singer notable for posing nude in *Playboy* in 68, who likewise had a parallel film career (including an appearance – with Elvis – in *Change of Habit*), together with Maria Rohm, as the victim, and Klaus Kinski.

The soundtrack, a very highly rated piece of psychedelic jazz, was done by Manfred Mann and Mike Hugg, with Mann also appearing in a jam session filmed in a cafe. Hugg wrote the material sung by McNair, whilst Darren's trumpet playing was dubbed by UK session man Henry Lowther. Uncredited assistance with various pieces of incidental music came from Stu Phillips, previously known for *The Monkees* TV series.

Maria Rohm and James Darren

Released August 1969, 86 minutes, colour
DVD: Released on Blue Underground, February 2005
SOUNDTRACK: Unreleased

THE STONES
IN THE PARK

Leslie Woodhead directs
The Rolling Stones star

The *World in Action* team at Granada TV – Jo Durden-Smith and Leslie Woodhead – diversified into music documentaries in the late 60s with a trio of memorable productions: *The Doors Are Open* (featuring The Doors at the Roundhouse), *Johnny Cash at San Quentin* and this, the famous 5 July 69 concert in Hyde Park that heralded the return to live gigs by The Rolling Stones after a two year hiatus and the debut of Mick Taylor, their replacement for Brian Jones.

Almost anthropological in tone, it provides an interesting and accurate record of the event, probably the best remembered of the mini festivals held in Hyde Park between 68 and 71.

Despite strong supporting performances on the same day from King Crimson and Family, it concentrates, unfortunately, almost entirely on the under rehearsed fourteen song set from the Stones. Marianne Faithfull and Paul McCartney are amongst those who can be seen in the background. There was no soundtrack release.

Jagger in action

BROADCAST: September 1969, 53 minutes, colour
DVD: Released by Granada Media, 2001
SOUNDTRACK: None released

MOON ZERO TWO

Roy Ward Baker directs
Don Ellis does the music

Catherine Schell looking like 1968 in 2028

Extreme optimism was a key ingredient of the 60s and early 70s: an automatic belief that technological progress would be benign, an acceptance of rapid change and the constant certainty of a better future. Inevitably, some of this was reflected in various TV and film productions of the era, most notably, for many people, the weekly BBC series *Tomorrow's World*, which ran from 65, attracting huge audiences. Featuring the latest gadgets and presented by Raymond Baxter, a former RAF fighter pilot (stuck in firmly positive mode throughout), it came with theme music from Johnny Dankworth. A December 67 episode even featured Pink Floyd and their light show.

Moon Zero Two, a drama set on a moon base in 2021, definitely belongs within this canon, taking place in a future lunar city where, naturally, a late 60s audience might anticipate their children would live. Here it turns out to be an elaborate structure with interiors that look suspiciously like something out of the 69 Ideal Home Exhibition. It even includes enough space for a discotheque featuring The Gojos, the dancers commonly seen on *Top of the Pops*. Billed as 'The Number One Space Western', it was made by Hammer as a serious attempt to compete with Kubrick's masterpiece *2001: A Space Odyssey* and was directed by Roy Ward Baker, whose many other credits included *Quatermass and The Pit*. The film cost £500,000 to make (approximately £35m today), most of this clearly being spent on the sets and design work rather than the cast headed by James Olson, Catherine Schell, Warren Mitchell (as the monocle wearing villain) and Adrienne Corri, none of whom was, or became, a major star. The plot involves something about a hijacked asteroid.

The score was done by US jazz rocker Don Ellis and includes an excellent title song by Julie Driscoll. Despite the contemporary standing of both Ellis and Driscoll, no soundtrack LP appears to have been forthcoming.

Released October 1969, 100 minutes, colour
DVD: Released by Warner Home Video, 2008
SOUNDTRACK: None released

PENSIERO D'AMORE

Mario Amendola directs
Mal stars and does the music

A number of UK pop acts – The Renegades, The Casuals, The Rokes – found themselves enjoying significantly greater popularity in Europe than at home during the 60s beat boom. Arguably the greatest of all though were Mal and The Primitives, who went from a very mid-range existence on the south Midlands ballroom circuit to mega stardom in Italy before seamlessly moving into pop films in *I Ragazzi di Bandiera Gialla* (68) alongside Italian band Equipe 84. Ruggedly handsome lead singer Paul Couling (aka Mal Ryder, or just Mal) was quickly singled out for a solo career. *Pensiero D'Amore* was his first cinematic venture and was very much a starring vehicle for him.

Written and directed by Mario Amendola, whose previous work included the spaghetti western *The Great Silence* (with Klaus Kinski and Jean-Louis Trintignant) and the period drama *Isabella – Duchessa dei Diavoli*, Paul/ Mal plays a handsome young English peer who decides to take a break hitchhiking across Europe – as any member of the House of Lords would – where he sings in restaurants and hotels and becomes famous. Silvia Dionisio, seen in many Italian pop musicals, co-stars.

The soundtrack was done by Mario Migliardi, best known (and highly regarded) today for his work on the trash epic *Tower of Screaming Virgins* and the spaghetti western *Renegade Gun*. It contains several contributions from Mal, the best known being the Italian language version of the Bee Gees song *'I've gotta get a message to you'*. This was number one in the Italian charts for four weeks in September 69 effortlessly outselling The Beatles and all comers in Italy. The film was so successful that it spawned *Lacrime d'amore*, a 70 sequel, of sorts, with the same team.

Released December 1969, 85 minutes, colour
DVD: No English language release available
SOUNDTRACK: None released.

THE MAGIC CHRISTIAN

Joe McGrath directs
Peter Sellers and Ringo Starr star

Raquel Welch and her devoted slaves

An independent production, whose huge extravagance reflected the view in the late 60s that no film consisting of Southern + Sellers + The Beatles could fail, *The Magic Christian* was directed by Joe McGrath, something of a pop movie expert after his work on *30 is a Dangerous Age, Cynthia* and *The Bliss of Mrs Blossom*. The script was based on the 59 Terry Southern satire about a man who thinks he can do anything – or get anything done – by use of money. The film relocated the plot to London and Southern, whose reputation was peaking at this point after his extraordinary successes with *Dr Strangelove, The Loved One, Barbarella, Candy* and *Easy Rider*, saw his storyline extensively rewritten by John Cleese and Graham Chapman.

The film stars Peter Sellers and Ringo Starr, alongside a huge and varied cast, many of whom – à la *Casino Royale* (another film that coincidentally involved Southern, McGrath and Sellers) appear only briefly. Critical reaction on its release was restrained, though, when viewed today, the end result is actually quite entertaining.

The soundtrack had a genesis as complex as the film's cast and production. It was originally announced that Denny Laine and Trevor Burton (who, when shooting started, were joining forces to launch the super group Balls) would provide the music. For reasons not clear, they were dropped from the project and replaced by Paul McCartney and fellow Apple label mates Badfinger. Laine and Burton maintained an interest, however, and released their version of the film title song (the Lennon and McCartney composition, *'If you want it (Come And Get It)'*) as The Magic Christians on Major Minor in November 69. Surprisingly, it flopped. A week later, Badfinger put out their recording on Apple, to coincide with the film's release, and it duly charted at number four in the UK and number seven in the US. It was then followed by the Badfinger LP *'Magic Christian Music'*, which contains the songs Badfinger perform in the film but not the soundtrack. This reached number fifty five in the US album charts. The official soundtrack finally appeared on Pye in April 70 (to modest sales), containing McCartney's compositions, as performed by Badfinger, and the Thunderclap Newman 69 megahit *'Something in the Air'*.

Released December 1969, 92 minutes, colour
DVD: Released by Republic Pictures, January 2003
SOUNDTRACK: Released on Pye, April 1970

ALL THE RIGHT NOISES

Gerry O'Hara directs
Olivia Hussey and Tom Bell star

One of a number of films that explored issues to do with the age of consent and contemporary permissiveness, *All the Right Noises* was written and directed by Gerry O'Hara, whose previous credits included the early Swinging London exploitation piece *The Pleasure Girls* and the crime capers *Maroc 7* and *Amsterdam Affair*. Production duties fell to Si Litvinoff, who would later be involved in a similar capacity with *A Clockwork Orange*, *Glastonbury Fayre* and *The Man Who Fell to Earth*.

Olivia Hussey

Here, a middle aged man with wife and children, played by Tom Bell (a reliable supporting actor and minor star in films such as *The L-Shaped Room*) finds himself infatuated with an underage Olivia Hussey, eighteen here but playing fifteen. This was Hussey's follow-up film to her huge 68 hit with *Romeo and Juliet* (in which she had been seventeen playing thirteen to ensure authenticity with Shakespeare's play) but, due to issues with the censor, *All the Right Noises* was nearly two years late reaching cinemas. It is regarded today as a well made UK minor feature of its time. A major supporting role was played by Judy Carne – famous for her appearances in *Rowan and Martin's Laugh-In* and identification with the catchphrase *'Sock it To Me'*… which she released as a novelty single at this time.

The soundtrack LP was done by Melanie, and, rather strangely, was one of her few recordings not to chart.

Released 1971 (filmed 1969), 92 minutes, colour
DVD: Released by BFI video, August 2009
SOUNDTRACK: Released on Buddah, July 1971

TILL DEATH
US DO PART

Warren Mitchell stars in a Johnny Speight script

The film version of the astonishingly successful 65-68 TV series expanded its traditional sitcom plot into a study of the Garnett family moving from poverty in the 30s, through the war and modest prosperity in the 50s to the changing social mores of the 60s. The cast are brilliant. Warren Mitchell stars as the ignorant, totemic working class head of the household, mouthing insulting and ludicrous opinions, which were deftly intended by his creator – Johnny Speight – to be the polar opposite of the apparently progressive and liberal values that underpinned 'Swinging London'. Dandy Nichols, an actress so popular during this period that she also had roles in *The Knack*, *Georgy Girl* and *The Bed Sitting Room*, appears as his long suffering and crushed wife. In support are Una Stubbs, whose career stretched back to the 50s TV rock and roll show *Cool for Cats* and the Cliff Richard musicals *Summer Holiday* and *Wonderful Life*, as Garnett's archetypal dolly bird daughter and Anthony Booth as his mouthy, layabout Liverpudlian son-in-law.

Mitchell's/Garnett's political and cultural rants were toned down for the big screen version, which was directed by Norman Cohen, whose other credits included a string of conventional – and coarse – comedies. The film works into its plot footage of the England 66 World Cup triumph and concludes with the demolition of the neighbourhood the Garnett family live in and their enforced transfer to a new home in a tower block in Essex.

Probably the first and best of the TV spin-offs the UK film industry produced through the 70s and 80s, *Till Death Us Do Part* came with a theme song written by Ray Davies, surely the ideal candidate to provide a song about the broad pageant of UK working class life and the melancholy behind the destruction of traditional communities. On screen it was sung by Chas Mills, a successful songwriter of the time who wrote hits for Peter and Gordon and Paul Jones, and who co-produced material with Mark Wirtz. Another version was released by Anthony Booth as a 45 on the Tangerine label.

Released 1969, 96 minutes, colour
DVD: Reissued on Elevation, May 2008
SOUNDTRACK LP/CD: No official release. The Kinks version of the film theme eventually appeared on *The Great Lost Kinks Album* on Reprise in January 1973, reaching number one hundred and forty five in the US chart

Kenny Lynch

If the US could produce global stars like Sammy Davis Jr., Sidney Poitier and Bill Cosby in the 60s... could the UK do similar from its black community?

The obvious candidate was Kenny Lynch, who grew up in a mixed race family in the East End of London and signed to EMI as a pop singer in 60. Pre-Beatles, he had a respectable career: scoring a hit with a cover of *'Up on the Roof'* in 62, this leading inevitably to slots in the compendium pop films *Just for Fun* and *Every Day's a Holiday*, for both of which he composed songs. The first person to cover a Lennon and McCartney song (*'Misery'* – March 63), he then knocked out part of the soundtrack of *Dr Terror's House of Horrors* and moved quickly into producing and arranging Dusty Springfield and some of the nascent mod groups from his own manor (The Game, The Boys, The Mark Leeman Five). The word that there was a UK performer who could write, arrange, produce and act a little reached across the Atlantic – presumably on the back of his cover of *'Up on the Roof'* and subsequent film work – and he was soon in a writing partnership with Mort Shuman and Jerry Ragovoy. This was elevated company indeed and quickly led to his greatest moment – co-writing, with Shuman, The Small Faces hit (*'Sha La La La Lee'*, number three in the UK charts in early 66). A purple patch followed, producing Cliff Bennett and The Rebel Rousers, Johnny Kidd and The Pirates, The Drifters, Herman's Hermits, Jimmy Winston, Cilla Black and the pre-Elton John Stu Brown and Bluesology, whilst honing his acting career with starring roles in two TV series: *Room at the Bottom* (66-67) with Kenneth Connor and Deryck Guyler and Spike Milligan's desperately, and deliberately, incorrect *Curry and Chips* (69), with Eric Sykes. The latter was Johnny Speight's riposte to Enoch Powell's 'rivers of blood' intervention in UK politics but, unlike *Till Death Us Do Part* (which was regarded with affection), was too close to the truth about the everyday reality of race relations and was pulled in mid production after a massive number of complaints to the Commission for Racial Equality.

It was strange, then, to come across him in *Carry on Loving* (70) – thirty sixth in the cast as a 'bus conductor'. Could the UK really find nothing better for him? Apparently not; and comparisons with, say, Bill Cosby – who during the same period was starring on TV in *I Spy*, running Tetragrammaton Records (and breaking Deep Purple and The Soft Machine in the US), commencing the mega popular *Bill Cosby Show* and launching a major film career – are striking. Despite a deal with Atlantic in 72 and continued success co-writing songs for The Hollies with Tony Hicks (five tracks on the *'Distant Light'* LP – a big hit in the US), Lynch soon languished into MOR tedium and TV guest slots when a comparable performer elsewhere would have had a string of high profile credits.

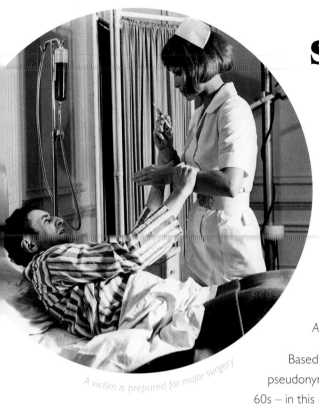
A victim is prepared for major surgery

SCREAM AND SCREAM AGAIN

Gordon Hessler directs
The Amen Corner do the music

One of a trio of horror films AIP made at this time in the UK as starring vehicles for Vincent Price, *Scream and Scream Again* was directed by Gordon Hessler, who began his career working with Alfred Hitchcock, and written by Christopher Wicking who, like Hessler, would accrue many horror credits and who counted among his later work the script for the 86 pop musical *Absolute Beginners*.

Based on the novel *The Disorientated Man* by Peter Saxon (a pseudonym used by several writers of horror/suspense tales in the 60s – in this case, the actual author was Stephen Frances who published a series of pulp works over many years), the plot concerns a scientist (Vincent Price) with markedly right wing and eugenicist views who is seeking to create a race of superhuman beings. One of his subjects escapes from his laboratory and rampages through the discotheques and night clubs of Swinging London, committing a series of gory murders. The supporting cast is headed by Christopher Lee, Peter Cushing, Judy Huxtable and Michael Gothard and the film is regarded today as energetic, well made and impressive.

Filmed in the late summer of 69, it includes several extended sequences of The Amen Corner performing the title song in what was virtually their last work before splitting up. The remainder of the soundtrack was entrusted to David Whitaker, who worked at this time with Blossom Toes, The Majority, Marianne Faithfull and Serge Gainsbourg.

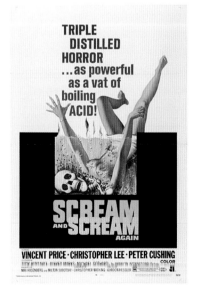

Released January 1970, 95 minutes, colour
DVD: Reissued by MGM in 2002
SOUNDTRACK LP/CD: Released on De Wolfe in 1994 with contributions from the Royal Philharmonic Orchestra.

TAKE A GIRL LIKE YOU

Jonathan Miller directs
Oliver Reed and Noel Harrison star in a George Melly script

One of a number of films with the typically 60s plot about the adventures of a young person (or people in some instances) leaving 'the North' and coming to London, *Take a Girl Like You* was the big screen adaptation of the popular 60 Kingsley Amis novel, in which a young girl arriving in the capital duly experiences difficulties dealing with various predatory males. It was the only film directed by Jonathan Miller, the legendary 60s satirist of *Beyond the Fringe* and theatre fame, and the second and final screenplay written by George Melly.

Filmed in and around Staines, Middlesex (i.e. near Shepperton Studios and thus saving production costs), Hayley Mills plays the young schoolteacher moving south. The male leads were taken by Oliver Reed and Noel Harrison – the latter a successful singer/actor of the time best known for his co-starring role in *The Girl from U.N.C.L.E.* and the hit single 'The Windmills of your Mind'. Eventually released as the lower part of a double bill, supporting the Elliott Gould campus comedy *Getting Straight*, *Take a Girl Like You* did not enjoy the commercial success that had attended earlier Amis adaptations such as *Lucky Jim* and *Only Two Can Play*.

The soundtrack was handled by Stanley Myers and includes a title song by The Foundations, several tracks from Ram John Holder and a contribution by vocal group Harmony Grass.

Released February 1970, 101 minutes, colour
DVD: Latest reissue on Sony, May 2010
SOUNDTRACK LP/CD: Released on Pye in 1970

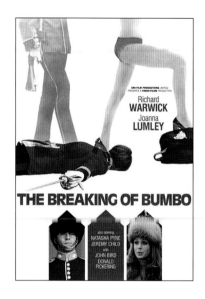

THE BREAKING OF BUMBO

Andrew Sinclair directs
Joanna Lumley stars

The Breaking of Bumbo takes a satirical look at the British Army and reflects the jaded views held by many people in the UK towards the military and traditional authority after the débacle of Suez and a string of minor colonial wars. It was adapted and directed, from his 59 novel, by Andrew Sinclair, one of the more curious figures of the period who, after a spell in the Guards, lectured in US history at University College London and wrote two books about Che Guevara.

The slightly bizarre plot concerns an army officer who tries to convert his regiment to pacifism. The modest cast is headed by Richard Warwick, previously a co-star in *If…* and Joanna Lumley. The film itself disappeared from circulation (apart from a few TV showings) after a premiere at the Roundhouse. Sinclair went on to do *Under Milk Wood* (72) with Burton and Taylor but rarely directed after the mid 70s.

One scene features The Graham Bond Initiation performing in a nightclub – the only surviving material from this stage of Bond's mercurial career, as the group broke up after thirty or so gigs, three radio shows and this film slot. They are briefly glimpsed playing *'Springtime in the City'*, released as a single by Bond in 70, but actually recorded some years earlier. The soundtrack was done by Brian Gascoigne, who also worked with The Scaffold, Blossom Dearie and Ralph McTell during this period.

Released 1970, 90 minutes, colour
DVD: Reissued by Network, September 2013
SOUNDTRACK LP/CD: No official release

The Name's Connery, Neil Connery...

The Bond films, with their brassy big band soundtracks and almost exclusively adult (as in middle-aged) casts, do not, as already stated elsewhere in this book, really serve as examples of 60s *pop* culture. Musically, Matt Monro and Shirley Bassey (not to mention Louis Armstrong) were stars long before The Beatles left Hamburg and their output was always aimed more at the mum and dad audiences than at the emerging youth market. But... the Bond franchise did establish trends in terms of plot, gadgets, design, general assumptions and fashion that were replicated by many other films and TV series and thus became common across youth orientated cinema.

The success of *Dr No* in the US triggered virtually everything that followed. Released there in May 63, by the end of the year it was one of the top ten grossing films: not bad for a low budget UK effort with a second string cast. With a surprised United Artists awash with box office takings, MGM and NBC promptly hired Ian Fleming to devise a plot for a series about an agent solving worldwide problems. Fleming

suggested Napoleon Solo... and thus began *The Man from U.N.C.L.E.*, which started filming in November 63 and ran from 64 to 68. On screen, Solo was supported by UK actor David McCallum (playing a Russian – U.N.C.L.E. was a secret global organisation) and, such was the immense popularity of the series, McCallum was soon receiving more fanmail than any other actor in the world. No less than eight feature film spin-offs emerged, the best of which was probably *The Karate Killers* (August 67), which has London sequences (in a night club,

naturally), albeit filmed in Hollywood, with an appearance by the US group Every Mother's Son, performing *'Come On Down To My Boat Baby'* – a track covered in the UK by The Gods. With U.N.C.L.E. clearly aimed more at teenagers than Bond, and being English a dead cert during Beatle mania, David McCallum signed a record deal with Capitol in late 65, scoring hits with his debut 45 *'Communication'* and LP *'Music: A Part of Me'* (number twenty four US, summer 66). There were several sequels, in which McCallum worked his way through the pop standards of the era.

The combined box office takings of Bond + U.N.C.L.E. immediately spawned further imitations. Twentieth Century Fox produced *Our Man Flint* (January 66, with James Coburn and a sequel) and Columbia put out *The Silencers* (February 66, with Dean Martin in the title role as Matt Helm and three sequels). Both films were in the US top twenty that year, and, like Solo, both Flint and Helm worked for secret

worldwide intelligence organisations. (Bond, of course, merely worked for Her Majesty's Government). The team behind Matt Helm also ventured to London to make *Hammerhead* (April 68), which opens with a US spy with a business suit, Jaguar and a Chelsea mews house hanging out at a counter-culture 'event' at the Roundhouse. Judy Geeson co-starred. Although, by comparison, Modesty Blaise was only a middling success, the UK also hosted MGM's *Casino Royale* (April 67) surely the greatest shambles of all – though still enjoyable – with six directors, ten screenplay writers and four Bonds: David Niven, Peter Sellers, Woody Allen and... Terence Cooper. Based on the only 007 book not optioned by Cubby Broccoli, it was a runaway success; as was *'The Look of Love'*, the Burt Bacharach song included on its soundtrack and performed by Dusty Springfield. Even odder – surreal even – was the Italian *OK Connery!* (April 67 too) which, complete with a blasting Shirley Bassey-style title song, featured Neil Connery, brother of Sean, as a bearded cosmetic surgeon and secret agent at the head of a cast that included Bernard Lee,

Lois Maxwell and Adolfo Celi from the main franchise. Other British *faux* Bonds included: *Deadlier Than the Male* (February 67), with Richard Johnson as Bulldog Drummond, a gentleman detective from the 20s now updated with a central London flat and sports car; sequel *Some Girls Do*, (January 69); *Danger Route* (October 67), Johnson again, as a licensed to kill MI6 agent; *Crossplot* (late 69) Roger Moore as an advertising executive with a central London flat and sports car fighting an attempt by a media baron to take over via a military coup; and even *Universal Soldier* (71) George Lazenby as a hippy Bond – with, at one point, a hovercraft – hanging out in Notting Hill with Germaine Greer. All were, in their own way, interesting productions with much attention paid to design, clothing and general ambience. And all had incomparable music: from The Walker Brothers, Lee Vanderbilt, Anita Harris, John Rowles and Phillip Goodhand-Tait respectively. Comparing the leading men, out of Johnson, Moore and Lazenby, Johnson probably made the most convincing 007 clone.

Peter Wyngarde as Jason King

TV also produced a wide range of spy/secret agent series clearly derived from Fleming's creation. In the US *The Girl from U.N.C.L.E.* ran from 66-67 (like Solo, its central character, April Dancer, had also been suggested by Fleming in 63). In McCallum's place as attractive English foil was Noel Harrison – who also enjoyed a parallel career as a folk/pop singer, culminating in his 69 hit 'The Windmills of your Mind'. The UK produced *The Prisoner* (67-68) which was original, serious and inscrutable (i.e. Kafkaesque); *The Champions* (68-69) which was low budget; and most striking of all *Department S* (69-70) and its sequel *Jason King* (71-72) featuring a central character – Jason King – as played by Peter Wyngarde, ridiculously attired and moustached, with literary pretensions and a jet-setting life style. Like McCallum and Harrison, Wyngarde also dipped his toe in pop waters, issuing his own eponymous LP on RCA in

Moore and Curtis

70, in which he declaimed his way through a variety of material, some of it in dubious taste. King would be regarded twenty years later as a seminal influence on Austin Powers. Ultimately there came, perhaps most appositely given real life espionage arrangements, two US/UK collaborations – *The Persuaders* (71-72) and *The Protectors* (72-73). The former had Roger Moore and Tony Curtis as globetrotting playboys, solving crimes that baffled conventional law and order agencies. The latter featured a post U.N.C.L.E. Napoleon Solo (Robert Vaughn), heading a London based secret outfit that 'protects the innocent'.

Gradually the cluster of Bond imitations fell away leaving, by the mid 70s, just the original franchise in business. Post Watergate it was difficult, perhaps, to sell the notion of a benign secret organisation. And, in the economic climate of the mid 70s, difficult to present plots featuring central characters with unexplained and opulent life styles. Curiously, though, one aspect of the 60s obsession with spies and secret agencies survived. Top secret global organisations that set the world to rights had always been a major device/conceit of US films and TV series. This was turned on its head from 75 with the appearance of the conspiracy theory document *The Skeleton Key to the Gemstone File* and the subsequent publicity, following its dissemination within the US and UK counter-culture, that it gave to various key personalities who allegedly orchestrated international events, notably Aristotle Onassis. Following *Gemstone*, many other conspiracy theories have appeared, featuring, for example, The Committee of 300, The Illuminati and The Bilderberg Group, some of these being real international groupings, some imagined. Today, the notion of the secret agent acting on behalf of shadowy secret international groupings remains a central part of conspiracy theories throughout the world, as well as a key plot device in thrillers, albeit far removed from Commander Bond and his 35 Bentley (subsequently upgraded to an Aston Martin DB5).

CONNECTING ROOMS

Michael Redgrave and Bette Davis star in a Hemdale production

A surprisingly hard film to track down, rarely seen and unavailable in any format, *Connecting Rooms* was the first production from Hemdale, the company formed by David Hemmings to fund good quality independent films and rock music (their ventures in this respect including early assistance in the careers of Yes and Black Sabbath). Based on a play, *The Cellist*, and shot in and around a dilapidated boarding house in Bayswater, and thus not dissimilar to earlier 'kitchen sink' dramas like *The L-Shaped Room*, *Connecting Rooms* starred Bette Davis and Michael Redgrave. The supporting cast was headed by Alexis Kanner, briefly a minor box office draw at this point following roles in *Crossplot* and *Goodbye Gemini*, who plays here an aspiring music industry hustler and song writer.

Gabrielle Drake

With much of the plot restricted to exchanges by the cast in a few rooms in a mostly dingy neighbourhood, the film is downbeat in tone and struggled to gain a commercial release: it premiered in the US in early 70 and had a few isolated cinema bookings in the UK in 72.

The soundtrack was entrusted to John Shakespeare (a.k.a. John Carter of The Ivy League) whose earlier film credits included much of the material featured in *Poor Cow*. In one sequence, the actress Olga Georges-Picot records one of Kanner's songs, her voice being dubbed by Lois Lane, a minor UK pop singer of the period, best known for being one half of The Caravelles. The Eyes of Blue also appear performing '*What Happens To Her*'.

Released 1970, 103 minutes, colour
DVD: Only bootleg copies available
SOUNDTRACK LP/CD: No official release

LET IT BE

Michael Lindsay-Hogg directs
The Beatles star

The Beatles bow out

Although The Beatles may have stopped touring in 66, their workload remained frenetic: 'Sgt.Pepper' and 'The White Album', a TV special, a feature cartoon and separate film projects for each group member… *The Family Way* (Paul), *How I Won the War* (John), *Wonderwall* (George) and *The Magic Christian* (Ringo – who also had a slot in *Candy*). In early 69, Paul McCartney made a determined attempt to reboot the group musically. Thus emerged *Let It Be*, an Apple Corps production which captures the group and its entourage (Yoko Ono, Linda McCartney, Billy Preston etc) in some disarray, recording the material for their next LP, intended at that point to be called *Get Back*, a title that reflected a conscious desire to return to their musical roots after the extravaganzas and travails of the preceding years.

Filmed in fly-on-the-wall documentary style by Michael Lindsay-Hogg, the end result shows the effects and mixed benefits of having an endless amount of studio time whilst being off the road for three years. The group stumble through a series of unimpressive sessions whilst arguing and bickering amongst themselves. A scene where Peter Sellers drops by for some jokey banter was immediately cut – most of the dialogue at this point concerning cannabis use. The remainder of the footage includes the impromptu rooftop concert given by The Beatles, an event that provides the most entertaining moments in the film and, in fact, proved to be their last live show.

McCartney brought in Glyn Johns, then hot as a result of his work on the debut Led Zeppelin LP, to produce the music. George Martin was retained, however, so Johns' role was unclear and ultimately limited. With the film in post-production and the group drifting on to the even more bitty *Abbey Road* sessions with Martin, the soundtrack was eventually dealt with by Phil Spector. By the time the film and accompanying LP appeared in May 70, the project (much remixed by Spector) had been renamed *Let It Be* and was chronologically the last Beatles release, appearing six months after the group's demise but still effortlessly reaching number one in most territories.

Released May 1970, 81 minutes, colour
DVD: Awaiting an official release
SOUNDTRACK LP/CD: Released on
Apple, May 1970

CANNABIS
(FRENCH INTRIGUE)

Pierre Koralnik directs
Serge Gainsbourg and Jane Birkin star

The second collaboration between Pierre Koralnik and Serge Gainsbourg after their 67 success with *Anna, Cannabis*, which was renamed *French Intrigue* in many countries due to its obviously risqué title, is a mafia thriller – a very popular genre in the 70s – about a hitman (a chain-smoking Gainsbourg) having an affair – with Jane Birkin – whilst going about his unpleasant duties. It was the third film starring the Birkin/Gainsbourg duo and appeared in the UK on the heels of their enormous number one hit single *'Je t'aime moi non plus'* (July 69), the completion of *Les Chemins de Katmandou (The Pleasure Pit)* and Birkin's solo role in *Alba pagana*.

Filmed on locations in New York and Paris, the film co-stars Paul Nicholas and Gabriele Ferzetti. Nicholas was a significant actor/pop singer who came to the role after playing one of the leads in the London stage production of *Hair*, whilst Ferzetti, with parts in *Better a Widow*, *Machine Gun McCain*, *Once Upon a Time in the West* and *On Her Majesty's Secret Service*, had one of the most colourful European CVs at this point.

Gainsbourg also did the film soundtrack, and, as can be expected, produced an elegant and highly regarded piece of work. Dedicated to Jimi Hendrix and Bartok, it was described many years later, when released as an LP, as resembling '… a Leonard Cohen concept realised over music borrowed from The Move's "Brontosaurus" …' Like all Gainsbourg's material, and most French crime thrillers, the end result is stylish and well made.

Birkin and Gainsbourg

Released May 1970, 95 minutes, colour
DVD: US release by Video Search of Miami 2009
SOUNDTRACK LP/CD: Released on Phillips, 1970

Exquisite Thing...

Who was the most successful actress to emerge from the UK pop cinema of the 60s?

Jane Birkin, by a long way. After *Wonderwall*, her first starring role, she appeared in seventeen feature films in six years and was top billed in three. None of her contemporaries could match this. Nor did any of the others have a number one hit, which she did with her 69 duet with Serge Gainsbourg *'Je t'aime moi non plus'*, an accomplishment that allowed her, from 73, to enjoy a parallel and successful career as a singer. Her family background prepared her admirably for this success. Judy Campbell, her mother, was a noted actress and singer in British films and theatre in the 40s, whilst her father served as an officer in naval intelligence in World War Two, during which, curiously, he knew Commander Ian Fleming, author of the Bond thrillers that later propelled John Barry (her first husband) to soundtrack stardom.

The key to Jane Birkin's brilliant career is that she never went cheap: not for her the sex comedies or tatty horror films offered to so many of her UK contemporaries (and accepted by so many). She remained a class act, very focussed on her work, avoiding the ravages of both heroin, that devastated Marianne Faithfull, and alcohol, that ultimately destroyed Gainsbourg.

Cineastes and musicophiles may detect a Birkin dynasty or even a Gainsbourg-Birkin *brand*. Andrew Birkin, her brother, though often in his sister's shadow, has also enjoyed a significant career: working straight from school on *Magical Mystery Tour* and *Popdown*, one of Kubrick's extensive crew on *2001: A Space Odyssey* and finally becoming a screenplay writer of some note with *The Pied Piper* (72). The baton today has surely passed to Jane's daughter, Charlotte Gainsbourg, who was inducted into the family business by her father at the age of twelve with their suitably provocative duet *'Lemon Incest'*, a number two hit in France despite (or because of) its association with paedophilia and incest. Since the early 90s, Charlotte has starred in films with William Hurt, Terence Stamp, Johnny Depp, Charlotte Rampling, Heath Ledger, Willem Dafoe, Kiefer Sutherland, Pete Doherty, Lily Cole and Jamie Bell. She has also released a number of albums including *'5.55'* with Jarvis Cocker (06) and *'IRM'* with Beck (09), both of which were considerable successes.

LOOT

Silvio Narizzano directs
Hywel Bennett stars

The career of Joe Orton paralleled that of The Beatles – he arrived in London from the provinces, had his commercial breakthrough in 63 and by 64-65 after West End hits with *Loot* and *Entertaining Mr Sloane* was rated the most exciting prospect to have emerged in UK theatre for a decade. Pop beckoned and in early 66 Walter Shenson asked him to provide a script for a third Beatles film. Developing the sub-Goonery of *Help!* even further, Orton produced *Up Against It!* in which the group arrive in London, accidentally become heroes in a civil war that breaks out in the UK and end up married – in a threesome – to the same young woman. Firmly rejected by Brian Epstein due to the gay/bisexual characterisations the script passed to Oscar Lewenstein, who saw it as a project starring Mick Jagger, with Richard Lester directing… only to collapse as a possibility with Orton's death in August 67.

Lee Remick, Joe Lynch and Hywel Bennett

Thus, the first film adaptation of his work to reach the cinemas was *Loot*, directed by Silvio Narizzano after his success with *Georgy Girl*. Ray Galton and Alan Simpson adapted the play, following their brilliant run in situation comedy with *Hancock* (spin off film – *The Rebel*) and *Steptoe and Son* (film – *The Bargee*) and a venture into TV pop specials with *Frankie Howerd meets the Bee Gees* (Thames TV August 68, co-stars Julie Driscoll and Brian Auger).

Shot in and around Brighton, the plot, a deliberately tasteless farce, concerns a gang of bank robbers storing the proceeds of their crimes in a coffin, requiring them to hide the corpse that it previously contained. The main roles were played by Lee Remick, Hywel Bennett and Richard Attenborough, the last as a police inspector. Remick and Attenborough made two films together at this time, the other being the matrimonial drama *A Severed Head*. A fine supporting cast includes Milo O'Shea and comedian Dick Emery, the latter having done voiceover work in *Yellow Submarine* as well as a supporting role in *Baby Love*. Generally reckoned to be a successful film, the soundtrack was by Keith Mansfield and includes an impressive title song sung by Steve Ellis.

Released May 1970, 101 minutes, colour
DVD: Released June 2005
SOUNDTRACK LP/CD: Released on CBS in 1970. Reissued on CD by RPM in 2001

Bronson and George

TWINKY
(LOLA)

Richard Donner directs
Charles Bronson and Susan
George star

After making *Salt and Pepper*, with
Sammy Davis Jr. and Peter Lawford
as Swinging London nightclub owners,
Richard Donner directed *Twinky*, which
has craggy Charles Bronson (forty nine
playing forty) as a dissolute and jaded writer
of pornographic novels shacking up with twee,
school-uniformed Susan George (nineteen playing
sixteen). Written by Norman Vane after he had scripted *Mrs
Brown, You've Got a Lovely Daughter*, it's yet another US excursion into
deepest Chelsea with a plot centred on the inappropriate and mildly
scandalous relationship between the two stars… one of several films at
this time that explored the dramatic potential of permissiveness and the
age of consent.

A heavyweight supporting cast is led by Trevor Howard, Honor Blackman
and Jack Hawkins and includes – in a minor role – Gordon Waller,
formerly one half of pop duo Peter and Gordon, as 'Marty the hippy'.

The soundtrack includes a breezy folk-pop theme song 'Twinky' written
and performed by Jim Dale and released as a single as early as June 69,
presumably in the hope that it would emulate his earlier success with
'Georgy Girl'.

Released May 1970, 98 minutes, colour
DVD: Reissued March 2006
SOUNDTRACK LP/CD: No release

GROUPIE GIRL

Derek Ford directs
Esme Johns stars

Supposedly a serious and hard-hitting realistic drama about the dangers awaiting young girls if they associated too closely with degenerate rock bands, *Groupie Girl* is actually a *News of The World* style exposé of the subject – presented in moral panic style – liberally decked out with a considerable amount of nudity, and, for the time, explicit sex scenes. The film was directed by Derek Ford, whose earlier career included the drama *Saturday Night Out* (64, with a featured role for The Searchers) but whose subsequent credits consisted exclusively of typical 70s and 80s UK sex films.

The cast is lightweight and includes a number of glamour girls of the period – Flanagan (the first topless model in a UK newspaper) and the Collinson twins, one time Playmates of the Month who later decorated a number of Hammer horror films. The lead role – of the groupie on the road to ruin – is played by Esme Johns, a stripper the producers found working in a club in Soho. It was her only film appearance. Filming took place in early 70, in rather bleak and unglamorous locations, and apparently included a number of orgy sequences that were cut from the UK cinema release, but were later shown – as still photographs – in *Mayfair* magazine. The rock bands being pursued so voraciously by their female admirers are played by Polydor recording acts Opal Butterfly and English Rose. Opal Butterfly included Ian 'Lemmy' Kilmister and Simon King, both later in Hawkwind, whilst English Rose were based around Lynton Guest, formerly the keyboard player in The Love Affair.

The remainder of the soundtrack was provided by Peter Lee Stirling and David Byron, Byron being in transit from late period psych group Spice to heavy rock dinosaurs Uriah Heep at this point. No formal release of the material appears to have taken place. One curiosity related to the film was the hit single enjoyed in the UK by Tony Joe White, whose song *'Groupie Girl'* reached number twenty two in the charts in June/July 70, despite being unconnected to the film but, perhaps, helped in its success by its release and notoriety.

Released 1 May 1970, 86 minutes, colour
DVD: Reissued on DVD by Slam Dunk Media in January 2007
SOUNDTRACK LP/CD: Released on Polydor in 1970. CD reissue on Screen Gold Records in 1997

AMOUGIES
(MUSIC POWER and EUROPEAN MUSIC REVOLUTION)

Jérôme Laperrousaz directs
Giorgio Gomelsky does the music

Zappa and Beefheart at Amougies

The first major European rock festival, held at Amougies, Belgium over five days in October 69, was organised by Giorgio Gomelsky and filmed for release as a documentary à la *Monterey Pop* by Jérôme Laperrousaz.

The cast was stellar: Ten Years After, Colosseum, Chicken Shack, East of Eden, The Pink Floyd, The Nice, Yes, The Pretty Things and The Soft Machine from the UK, Daevid Allen's Gong and Zoo from France, Frank Zappa and Captain Beefheart and The Magic Band from the US, together with a substantial jazz element led by Don Cherry and Pharoah Sanders. Zappa was brought across by Gomelsky as a compère for the event, but, accompanied by Beefheart (on his first visit to Europe), ended up jamming with many of the artists.

When edited the completed work was over 4 hours long and ended up being shown as two separate films: *Music Power* and *European Music Revolution*. Not that cinema screenings lasted very long. Lawyers acting for The Pink Floyd quickly served an injunction (citing copyright – the group had been booked to play, not to play *and* be filmed) that stopped further showings. Some commentators have speculated that they may have been concerned about the footage of them performing 'Interstellar Overdrive' with Frank Zappa on guitar: an event they later claimed to have forgotten and which many consider to be the high point of the film. Given that when the Amougies Festival was held they had not yet fully recovered in Europe the standing the group had enjoyed in 67 when led by Syd Barrett, whose guitar work on the same track was pivotal, this may have been of some significance.

The absence to this day of either a legitimate film or soundtrack release makes the work as a whole difficult to judge. However, it is remembered as being an interesting document of its time with many fine musical interludes, despite being filmed in difficult circumstances.

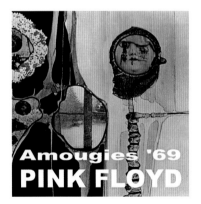

Released May 1970, 215 minutes
(combined running time of two films
when released), colour
DVD: Film withdrawn 1970.
No subsequent official release
SOUNDTRACK: No official release
various bootleg recordings in circulation

EYEWITNESS

John Hough directs
Mark Lester stars

The first film directed by John Hough, who went on to do sterling work on a number of Hammer horrors, *Eyewitness* (aka *Sudden Terror*) is a well made and entertaining political thriller, scripted by Ronald Harwood and shot on location in Malta. The plot has echoes of Hitchcock: a young boy (Mark Lester) is the only witness to the assassination of a visiting African leader, and subsequently struggles to escape retribution from the perpetrators.

Lester, after huge successes in *Oliver* and *Run Wild, Run Free* in 68-69, was evidently deemed suitable to carry the leading role in a largely adult film, despite being only twelve years old at the time. Lionel Jeffries and Susan George co-star, George appearing here after roles in *Up the Junction*, *Twinky* and the late 'kitchen sink' drama *Spring and Port Wine*.

The film came with an elaborate and carefully assembled soundtrack that was produced by Jonathan Demme from songs selected by Dave Symonds, a Radio One DJ and manager of Fairfield Parlour. Not surprisingly, Fairfield Parlour got to sing the title theme, *'Eyewitness'*, which was released as a single in Japan. In addition to this, Van der Graaf Generator contributed eight songs – virtually an album's worth of material – to the score, not all of which were used subsequently. No full length soundtrack LP was released.

Released June 1070, 91 minutes, colour
DVD: Reissued via Network, March 2010
SOUNDTRACK LP/CD: None released

GOODBYE GEMINI

Alan Gibson directs
Judy Geeson stars

One of a number of horror films/thrillers set against the backdrop of Swinging London, *Goodbye Gemini* was a carefully made but rather modest production whose main selling point was its star Judy Geeson, appearing here in a third major role following *To Sir, With Love* and *Here We Go Round the Mulberry Bush*.

Dissolute behaviour by the inhabitants of the posh bits of London had been a plot device for some time by this point, notably in *The Servant* (63) and *Darling* (65), a trend – possibly – reflecting an interest in such matters in the wake of the Profumo scandal. Here the film is about some 'unnaturally close' jet-setting twins (Geeson and co-star Martin Potter) who get mixed up in orgies and similar antics in Chelsea, with predictably disastrous consequences. Potter had just appeared in Fellini's *Satyricon* (69) – set in ancient Rome and like this featuring a great deal of wayward conduct. Michael Redgrave and Alexis Kanner co-star, both having graced *Connecting Rooms* only a few months earlier. The supporting cast is led by Mike Pratt, whose career proceeded from writing early rock and roll hits for Tommy Steele via doing the soundtracks for *The System* and *The Party's Over* to starring in the TV series *Randall and Hopkirk (Deceased)*.

The soundtrack includes a title song from Jackie Lee and contributions from both The Peddlers and Peter Lee Stirling.

Released July 1970, 89 minutes, colour
DVD: Reissued via DB Music Sales, May 2010
SOUNDTRACK LP/CD: Released on DJM in 1970.
Reissued on CD by Harkit Records, 2005

THIS, THAT AND THE OTHER!

Derek Ford directs
Dennis Waterman and Victor Spinetti star

A portmanteau film, made at a time when portmanteau films were a frequent and popular item in cinemas, *This, That and The Other!* (also known as *A Promise of Bed*) contains three separate sex comedy stories.

Directed by Derek Ford, whose career moved from this (and his earlier *Groupie Girl*) downwards through a long list of UK sex films in the 70s and 80s, the different episodes star Victor Spinetti, a stalwart companion of The Beatles in *A Hard Day's Night*, *Help!* and *Magical Mystery Tour*, as a suicidal man rescued from his fate by being invited to a party; Dennis Waterman, as a photographer (a common occupation on the screen post-*Blow-Up*); and John Bird, as a sex-obsessed taxi driver. The leading female role was taken by Vanessa Howard, whose other appearances at this time included *Here We Go Round the Mulberry Bush*, *Some Girls Do*, *Mumsy, Nanny, Sonny and Girly* and *The Rise and Rise of Michael Rimmer*. The production values are high and the film boasts some interesting and distinctive psychedelic photography.

Dennis Waterman and co-stars

The soundtrack was credited to a minor pop group, Scrugg, whose lead singer and guitarist, John Kongos, later achieved solo success with his 71 hit 'He's Gonna Step on You Again' and whose drummer, Henry Spinetti (brother of Victor), also featured in Mayfield's Mule, another now forgotten ensemble of the period.

Scrugg

Released July 1970, 78 Minutes, colour
DVD: Reissued via Odeon Entertainment, February 2010
SOUNDTRACK LP/CD: No official release

ENTERTAINING MR SLOANE

Douglas Hickox directs
Peter McEnery stars
Georgie Fame does the music

Andrews, McEnery and Reid

The second cinema adaptation of a Joe Orton play to appear in 70, *Entertaining Mr Sloane* was directed by Douglas Hickox, whose career had begun with the pop musicals *It's All Over Town* and *Just for Fun*. The script was by Clive Exton, who had done uncredited work on *Georgy Girl* as well as *Isadora* and *10 Rillington Place*. It followed a 68 TV adaptation, scripted by Orton himself shortly before his murder, which had starred Clive Francis, later seen in *Girl Stroke Boy*.

A considerable *tour de force* of bad taste, the plot concerns a young man, Peter McEnery, who moves in with a brother and sister (both in late middle age) played by Beryl Reid and Harry Andrews, causing sexual mayhem in the process. The ensemble playing of the main cast figures is particularly effective. With hindsight, it is curious to note, when watching it now, the career of McEnery, and how it seems almost emblematic of the era: an enviable CV with a steady stream of major roles (*Victim*, *The Game is Over*, *Negatives*, *Better a Widow* and *The Adventures of Gerard*) before lapsing into semi-obscurity.

Filmed against the Victorian gothic backdrop of Camberwell Cemetery, and the surrounding south London streets of Brockley, the film includes a quiet, slightly melancholy and understated theme song by Georgie Fame who, with his colleague from The Blue Flames, Colin Green, did the soundtrack. Green would later switch to Alan Price's backing band for *O Lucky Man!* and work on the score of *Psychomania*.

Released 27 July 1970, 94 minutes, colour
DVD: Reissued via Cinema Club, June 2005
SOUNDTRACK LP/CD: None released

ALBA PAGANA
(MAY MORNING)

Ugo Liberatore directs
Jane Birkin stars
The Tremeloes do the music

An Italian feature shot in the UK, *Alba pagana* was one of several films directed by Ugo Liberatore that mixed sex, nudity and murder in exotic locations... his 68 work *The Sex of Angels/Il sesso degli angeli*, for instance, has a boatload of women becalmed in the Adriatic tripping on LSD. *Alba pagana* was his Swinging London piece, albeit relocated to Oxford. Curiously, despite having provided his own screenplay for *The Idol* (66 – with pop star John Leyton and music from Johnny Dankworth), he used here a script by George Crowther, a minor actor previously best known for playing a series of supporting roles in *Hancock's Half Hour*.

The story concerns a foreign student (Alessio Orano) experiencing, as an outsider, the strange rituals and ceremonies of a traditional UK university town and the rather sinister outcome that these can have. The female lead was played by Jane Birkin – then a hot property in the UK following her appearance in *Wonderwall* and her 69 duet with Serge Gainsbourg *'Je t'aime moi non plus'* – who obligingly appears nude in a number of scenes. The supporting cast was led by John Steiner, a UK actor who had a big career in Italy including an appearance, during this period, in the spaghetti western *Tepepa* with Orson Welles and Tomas Milian.

The score was entrusted to Armando Trovajoli, the third occasion he worked on a UK based film, the others being *Col cuore in gola* and *Sette volte Sette*. He commissioned The Tremeloes, who at this point were attempting to move away from their mainstream pop image towards a sound more akin to that of The Band or Crosby, Stills, Nash and Young, to compose and perform much of the film soundtrack. They duly produced a complete album of material for this purpose.

Alba pagana had only a limited UK release and did not appear in the US until 72, by which time it had been renamed *May Morning*. Either because of this, or due to the failure of The Tremeloes' simultaneous attempt at a 'serious' rock LP (*'Master'*), the soundtrack remained unreleased for many years.

Released August 1970, 101 minutes, colour
DVD: Released by VCI Video, January 2000
SOUNDTRACK LP/CD: Released 2004

THE BEAST IN THE CELLAR

James Kelley directs
Tony Macaulay does the music

Connoisseurs of the Italian 'giallo' genre films that appeared in the 60s and 70s, with their lively innovative use of horror, suspense, violent crime, explicit sexuality and distinctive theme music, could well conclude that Tigon Films were the only UK production company that came anywhere near matching this creativity. After *What's Good for the Goose* and *The Haunted House of Horror*, this was their third venture to include a significant element of pop music.

One of the few films directed by James Kelley, a TV scriptwriter, it has a straightforward plot familiar to connoisseurs of UK horror: strange murders are happening on the moors and the police are baffled. Beryl Reid and Flora Robson star as sisters who have kept their brother locked in the cellar for thirty plus years. He escapes, and…

Much to the anger of its stars, the film was subject to post-production cuts and the coherence of the storyline compromised as a result. Kelley would direct only one more film, *Night Hair Child* (71), with Mark Lester and Britt Ekland, the credits for which list Andrea Bianchi – a consummate giallist – as co-director.

The soundtrack was done by Tony Macaulay, writer of numerous hits for The Marmalade, Long John Baldry and The Foundations. It includes Edison Lighthouse singing the theme song *'She Works In A Woman's Way'*.

Released August 1970, 101 minutes, colour
DVD: Reissued via Anchor Bay in July 2005
SOUNDTRACK LP/CD: None released

BRONCO BULLFROG

Barney Platts-Mills directs
Audience do the music

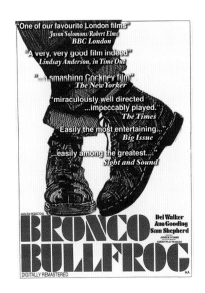

Very much the other side of Swinging London, *Bronco Bullfrog* is a gritty, neo-realist working class drama filmed away from the locations normally favoured by 60s cinema (Chelsea and Notting Hill Gate etc) and is set instead in West Ham and Stratford.

Possibly the last feature to be shot in black and white, it was made in 69 and released a year later. Directed by Barney Platts-Mills, the various acting roles were played by the young members of a local community theatre group, most of whom did not enjoy subsequent careers. The plot follows the escapades of local juvenile delinquents, many of whom are suedeheads or skinheads in the fashion of the time. A decidedly down to earth return to reality in its portrayal of the working classes (unlike, say, the romanticised version shown in films like *Up the Junction*) it could be said to be the prototype for the various dramas directed by Mike Leigh from 71 onwards.

The soundtrack was provided by Audience, an early 'progressive' group. Formed by two Hackney born musicians, Howard Werth and Keith Gemmell, Audience had emerged from the seven piece soul band The Lloyd Alexander Real Estate and, at that point, had just been signed by Polydor.

Del Walker and Anne Gooding

Released August 1970, 86 minutes,
black and white
DVD: Reissued by BFI, September 2010
SOUNDTRACK: CD issued in 2003 on RPM.
Several tracks by Audience appear on their
1969 debut LP on Polydor

LEO THE LAST

John Boorman directs
Marcello Mastroianni and Billie Whitelaw star

Marcello Mastroianni

An early John Boorman film, *Leo the Last* is a surreal and allegorical account of an exiled European royal, who, with his rather odd retinue and collection of retainers, decides to move back to a property his family once owned – in better times – in north Kensington. He does so, but finds that his once fashionable house in a formerly elegant part of London is now a down-at-heel property in a multicultural slum. Although some critics felt that Boorman's film was excessively mannered, in judging just how surreal, or realistic (or not), it might have been it is worth remembering that, in 69, much of the Latimer Road location where it was shot was empty and awaiting demolition and had been squatted by counter-cultural elements who temporarily renamed it 'Frestonia', whilst several shadowy 'Governments in Exile', some of which dated back to the 30s, did indeed have diplomatic residencies in or near the area. In addition, the sudden proliferation in the 60s of West Indian, African and Asian communities within such a run down and transient setting did seem, not least to much of the host population, to be deeply alien at the time.

Marcello Mastroianni and Billie Whitelaw star, with support from Calvin Lockhart and Glenna Forster-Jones (both seen in *Joanna*). Ram John Holder is credited with providing 'additional script material' for the film which, to a degree, explores similar themes, in a similar part of town, to those written about by him on his 70 LP *'Black London Blues'*. The film features brilliantly hallucinatory photography, particularly during its opening sequence set in a rain storm with an array of faces floating *'Sgt. Pepper'* style in front of the camera against the derelict backdrop and is clearly influenced by Fellini. Mastroianni appears to represent a decent but ineffectual aristocratic leader in a malevolent world, in which his retainers are a useless parasitical upper class and the largely black/immigrant community is portrayed either as hip, highly Americanised gangsters or oppressed downtrodden workers.

The soundtrack was done by Fred Myrow, who worked with US folk singer David Ackles, but was restricted to a Ram John Holder single release on United Artists. *Leo the Last* won Boorman a best director prize at the 70 Cannes Film Festival but was not a commercial success.

Released September 1970,
104 minutes, colour
DVD: Not available
SOUNDTRACK LP/CD: None released

DEEP END

Jerzy Skolimowski directs
Jane Asher stars

Directed by Jerzy Skolimowski and
filmed on location in Bavaria with a mainly
German cast (though set in London), *Deep
End* is a film about a fifteen-year-old boy who
gets a job in his local swimming baths and becomes
infatuated by one of the young women working there.

Both leading roles were taken by former child stars of the
UK cinema: Jane Asher, formerly Paul McCartney's girlfriend, and John
Moulder-Brown. The main supporting role was played by Chris Sandford
– another child star of the 50s and 60s, whose subsequent career included
spells as a successful pop singer and a Radio Caroline DJ.

John Moulder-Brown and Jane Asher

The film premiered at the 70 Venice Film Festival and came with a
soundtrack that included contributions from Can and Cat Stevens. It was
rated an artistic and commercial success, so much so that producer Lutz
Hengst got US funding for his next project – *King, Queen, Knave* – made
with David Wolper of *If It's Tuesday, This Must Be Belgium*. Like *Deep End*
this was directed by Skolimowski and had Moulder-Brown and Sandford
in the cast, with electronic music, in this instance, provided by Francis
Monkman of Curved Air. It has yet to be revived with anywhere near the
standing of the former film though.

Released September 1970, 90 minutes, colour
DVD: Reissued via Lace Group July 2011
SOUNDTRACK LP/CD: Some of the contribution from Can appears on their LP
Soundtracks released in West Germany on Liberty in 1970 and on United Artists in
the UK in 1973 and subsequently reissued in CD format in the UK on Spoon in 2004

Mick Jagger as Turner

PERFORMANCE

Donald Cammell and Nicolas Roeg direct
Mick Jagger, James Fox and Anita Pallenberg star

Filmed in the summer of 68, Warner Brothers initially approached *Performance* with something akin to enthusiasm: it had a US producer, resident in London (Sanford Lieberson), the director, Donald Cammell, had previously turned out two interesting scripts, *Duffy* and *The Touchables*, the cinematographer, Nicolas Roeg, had just returned from shooting *Petulia*, they were making a crime caper with a UK star, James Fox, supported by two bankable US actresses, Tuesday Weld and Mia Farrow and – to catch the youth market – Mick Jagger, lead singer of The Rolling Stones, was co-starring.

As things happened, it didn't quite work out that way. Both Weld and Farrow turned out to be unavailable and were replaced by Anita Pallenberg, just noticed in a major role in *Barbarella*, and Michele Breton, whose slender credits mainly consisted of an appearance in the Italian/French/German TV series *Odissea*. The plot, which has echoes of the career and demise of the Kray brothers (whose trial and conviction took place during this time and at which, in a strange coincidence, they were defended by John Platts-Mills QC, the father of the director of *Bronco Bullfrog*), concerns a vicious criminal (Fox) hiding out with a faded rock star (Jagger), with two hippy girlfriends (Pallenberg and Breton), after taking part in a botched murder. Unusually, the gangsters, the most significant of whom were John Bindon (from *Poor Cow*) and Johnny Shannon, a south London man who'd grown up among criminals, are shown as matter of fact, confident, fashionable, ultraviolent and basically… rather stylish. Their performances are neither mannered nor actorly nor unduly class conscious and set the template that has been followed ever since for this type of role.

Shooting was finished relatively quickly but the post-production work was troubled. Cammell dropped out and was replaced by Roeg, with the film not appearing until 70 and eventually costing £750,000 (equivalent to £21m today) — an enormous sum for something with a less than stellar cast and sets that consisted mainly of interiors. Even the locations had a fascinating back story. Two houses were used for the main scenes. One, in Lowndes Square, was the former London residence of Leonard Plugge, the owner for many years of Radio Luxembourg, and a considerable figure in the London social world from the 30s through to the 70s. The other, in Powis Square, Notting Hill (where Brian Jones had lived some years earlier) was later the home of John Barker, an activist in The Angry Brigade, considered at the time to be the closest equivalent in the UK to a counter-culture terrorist group of the type found in West Germany with the Baader-Meinhof Gang. (They bombed the Miss World contest.) The brilliantly dreamy photography, talkative script and continual use of music throughout the film are reminiscent of a Scorsese production and, given that *Performance* predated his first major work by more than two years, one wonders to what extent he was influenced by Cammell and Roeg.

Warners were duly dismayed at the darkness of the finished product, and at how English it was. But the combination of sex plus drugs plus

Anita and Mick

violence plus trippy soundtrack (eventually) made *Performance* a commercial success, and a staple of late night cinema and TV screenings for decades afterwards. Some have claimed that the strain and moral ambiguity felt by some of the participants whilst filming had a sombre legacy. It is far from clear that this was so. Although Michele Breton disappeared from view, and James Fox found personal salvation in Christianity and didn't film again for ten years, Anita Pallenberg co-starred in the Italian *Dillinger e morto* before drug problems claimed her and Jagger went to Australia to make *Ned Kelly*. Cammell, beset too by drug issues, eventually managed to get MGM to back *Demon Seed*. Both Roeg and Lieberson became major figures: Roeg with *Walkabout*, *Glastonbury Fayre* (which Lieberson also produced), *Don't Look Now*, *The Man Who Fell to Earth* and *Bad Timing*; Lieberson with *The Rolling Stones Rock and Roll Circus* (another troubled project with Jagger), *The Pied Piper*, *That'll Be the Day*, *The Final Programme*, *Mahler*, *Stardust*, *Lisztomania* and *Jabberwocky*. The gangsters also moved on to other work… Shannon and Bindon were both in the ITV crime series *The Gold Robbers*, with Shannon later appearing in *Slade in Flame*.

The soundtrack was put together by Jack Nitzsche who had just finished scoring *Bullitt* and whose work included producing PJ Proby, The Walker Brothers and Buffalo Springfield and arranging the Ike and Tina Turner classic 'River Deep, Mountain High'. It features material by Merry Clayton, The Last Poets, Randy Newman and Buffy Sainte-Marie. Curiously, given that *Performance* is a very English film, the fact that the accompanying music was mainly American does not detract from its appropriateness or impact. Mick Jagger's rendition of 'Memo from Turner', a key scene in the film, was released as a single and provided him with a minor hit.

A classic.

Released September 1970, 105 minutes, colour
DVD: Reissued via Warner Home Video, March 2006
SOUNDTRACK LP/CD: Released on Warner Brothers, September 1970. Reissued in CD format, 2003

DADDY, DARLING

Joseph Sarno directs
Tony Hazzard does the music

Directed by Joseph Sarno, who was responsible for dozens of US sex exploitation films (he racked up no fewer than forty four directing credits between 67 and 77), *Daddy, Darling* was a fairly typical Scandinavian feature of its type – an adult drama with substantial amounts of nudity and, for the time, explicit sex. Made after he completed *The Indelicate Balance* in Sweden, some European critics consider it the best of Sarno's films.

The plot involves a teenage girl who lives with her father and who takes umbrage after he rejects her incestuous advances and introduces her to his new girlfriend, and future stepmother. The lead roles were played by Helli Louise, a minor Danish actress later seen in 70s UK films such as *Confessions of a Pop Performer,* and Gio Petré whose career in Swedish cinema included starring roles in *The Doll* (62), *Loving Couples* (64 – music by Roger Wallis of Science Poption), *The Cats* (65), *I, a Woman Part 2* (68) and *Ann and Eve* (69). Unlike Liv Ullmann or Ewa Aulin, though, her career remained within Scandinavia and *Daddy, Darling* turned out to be her last film before she retired.

The soundtrack includes a number of songs featured on the 69 LP *'Tony Hazzard Sings Tony Hazzard'*, Hazzard being a songwriter of note who composed hits for Herman's Hermits, Gene Pitney, Lulu, Manfred Mann and The Tremeloes.

Released November 1970, 95 minutes (cut to 83 minutes for UK release), colour
DVD: Reissued via Ryko Distribution, July 2008
SOUNDTRACK LP/CD: None released

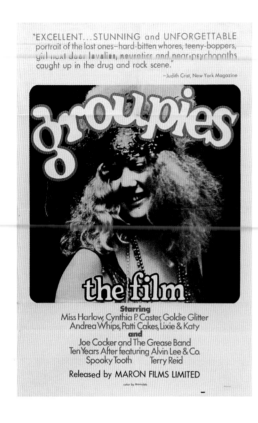

"EXCELLENT...STUNNING and UNFORGETTABLE portrait of the lost ones—hard-bitten whores, teeny-boppers, girl next door lovelies, neurotics and near-psychopaths caught up in the drug and rock scene."
–Judith Crist, New York Magazine

groupies
the film

Starring
Miss Harlow, Cynthia P. Caster, Goldie Glitter
Andrea Whips, Patti Cakes, Lixie & Katy
and
Joe Cocker and The Grease Band
Ten Years After featuring Alvin Lee & Co.
Spooky Tooth   Terry Reid

Released by MARON FILMS LIMITED

color by Movielab

GROUPIES

Ron Dorfman and Peter Nevard direct
various UK rock artists appear

The groupie phenomenon was certainly well to the fore in 70, and was clearly seen in some quarters as having commercial potential. As well as the UK film, the Tony Joe White hit single (and even a spoken word LP, released on Earth in the US, on which various teenagers relate their experiences), interest in the subject also spawned a US film documentary, *Groupies*, made by cine-photographers Ron Dorfman and Peter Nevard, about the adventures of various British groups touring the American ballroom and college circuit. Dorfman's career rarely strayed from sex films; Nevard, however, would later shoot the 79 documentary *The Kids Are Alright* about the career of The Who.

It includes concert sequences shot at the Fillmore and features both female and male groupies, hanging around hopefully in anticipation of being able to tempt some of the rock stars. Among those on display are Andrea Whips, aka Andrea Feldman, from Andy Warhol's Factory, and Cynthia Plaster Caster who, notoriously, assembled a collection of plaster casts of erect male genitalia.

Joe Cocker and The Grease Band, Ten Years After, Spooky Tooth and Terry Reid are the acts on view, all of them being arguably at the pinnacle of their fame at around this time.

Released November 1970, 92 minutes, colour
DVD: Reissued via Cherry Red in December 2001
SOUNDTRACK LP/CD: None released

THE BODY

Tony Garnett produces
Ron Geesin and Pink Floyd do the music

If there was such a thing as left wing cinema in the UK during the Swinging London era, this was one of its major productions – a documentary about the human body, and how various bits of it work. An adaptation of a 68 Anthony Smith bestseller, it was scripted by Adrian Mitchell, a socialist/pacifist poet of some renown, who, whilst covering pop music for *The Daily Mail* in 62, published the first national interview with The Beatles and went on to write the screenplay for *Marat/Sade* (67), the 68 TV special *Georgia Brown Sings Kurt Weill* and an important adaptation of *Man Friday* (72 – with Ram John Holder and Colin Blakely) in which the characteristics of the main players are reversed: black man wise and clever… white man stupid.

The film was Tony Garnett's follow-up project to *Kes*. Garnett began his career as an actor (he was one of the delinquents, alongside pop star Jess Conrad, in the 62 courtroom drama *The Boys*) but then moved behind the camera as story editor for the 65 TV production of *Up the Junction*, before making his reputation by producing the monumentally influential *Cathy Come Home* (66). *The Big Flame*, another major TV play, established his left wing credentials: a drama about the crushing of a hopeless strike in Liverpool, written by Jim Allen, a member of the Socialist Labour League (SLL)… a grouping it might be fair to call extremist. (*The Big Flame* was so highly regarded that a libertarian socialist faction named themselves after it). After this Garnett, via Kestrel Films, spent £150,000 making *Kes*, his first film, and scored a critical and commercial success… so much so that EMI agreed to distribute *The Body*. Directed by Roy Battersby and narrated by Vanessa Redgrave (who, like Battersby and Jim Allen, was also a member of the

SLL), it included a solemnly presented sequence where Richard Neville – the then editor of *Oz* magazine – has sex with his girlfriend. Looked at today, the popularity of a manual describing bodily functions (a trend that also produced, during this period, *The Joy of Sex*) and the perceived existence of a cinema audience for such material in 70 clearly marks it out as a product of an era where experimentation and optimism were regarded as the norm. It's not clear today what the box office returns for the film actually were… but it is an archetypal example of the type of fare presented at student union and college film societies and independent cinemas during the period.

The soundtrack was done by Ron Geesin, an avant-garde composer linked at the time to Pink Floyd, and includes *inter alia* some of his ragtime piano work. He is assisted by Roger Waters, and on one track by the other members of the group. The majority of the music was assembled from sounds made by the human body – burps, farts, coughs, sneezes, heartbeats, human voices, general stomach noises etc. Kestrel Films followed *The Body* with *Family Life*, a grim 71 drama directed by Ken Loach, from a David Mercer script, about a young woman being treated for mental health problems, with a soundtrack by Marc Wilkinson, who had also scored *If…* Roy Battersby would later work with Colin Welland, who appeared as an actor in *Kes*, on the 74 TV drama *Leeds United* (another story about a strike) but left wing cinema never took off in the UK and, in 80, Garnett quit to live and work in Los Angeles.

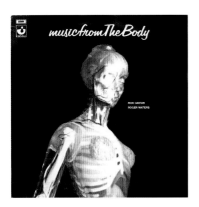

Released November 1970, 112 minutes, colour
DVD. Reissued on Warner Brothers
SOUNDTRACK LP/CD: Released on Harvest in 1970. CD reissue on Harvest 1989

GIMME SHELTER

Albert and David Maysles direct
The Rolling Stones star

A documentary from the respected team
of Albert and David Maysles, *Gimme Shelter*
follows The Rolling Stones on their tour of
the US in the summer and autumn of 69,
culminating in the notorious gig at Altamont.

Prior to making this, Albert Maysles had been
cameraman on *What's Happening! The Beatles in
the USA* (TV, 64) and *Monterey Pop* (68). His crisp
professional style and eye for striking images is evident
here throughout and he can claim, given his non music
credits – *The Delegate* (64, with Nixon and Goldwater),
Meet Marlon Brando (66), *With Love from Truman* (Capote, 67) –
to be one of several people who 'shot' the 60s. A very Jagger-centric
view of events – he features a great deal – various supporting acts on the
same tour, including Jefferson Airplane, The Flying Burrito Brothers and
Ike and Tina Turner are also glimpsed in action.

Because of its success as a cinema release, Decca subsequently put out an
LP with the same title in September 71 (which reached number nineteen
in the UK chart)… but this was a purely exploitative move by them: it
contained material previously released or recorded some years earlier.
There was no official soundtrack LP.

Jagger at Altamont

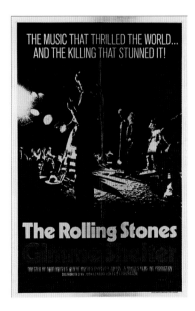

Released December 1970, 91 minutes, colour
DVD: Reissued via Warner Home Video
SOUNDTRACK LP/CD: Available in bootleg from 1973

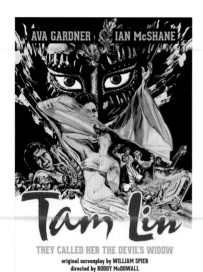

AVA GARDNER · IAN McSHANE

Tam Lin

THEY CALLED HER THE DEVIL'S WIDOW

original screenplay by WILLIAM SPIER
directed by RODDY McDOWALL

THE BALLAD OF TAM LIN

Roddy McDowall directs
Ian McShane and Ava Gardner star
Pentangle do the music

Opening with a sequence in which a group of Swinging London hangers-on tumble into a convoy of cars somewhere in Chelsea and then drive north in convoy, headed by Ian McShane and Ava Gardner in an open top Rolls-Royce, *Tam Lin* was a contemporary retelling of an old Scottish ballad, shot in 69 on location near the small town of Peebles. A well produced and acted horror film directed by Roddy McDowall (who as a young man had appeared in Orson Welles' brilliantly improvised film of *Macbeth*), with a script from US TV writer William Spier, the setting, plot about diabolical or pagan powers, and dreamy contemporary music make it something of a precursor to *The Wicker Man*, a film made some years later which, like this production, took a while to become fully appreciated.

Ava Gardner stars as an ageing woman who uses witchcraft to control the group of decadent young people (the film is set in the present) with whom she deliberately surrounds herself. Ian McShane heads a strong British supporting cast, in which, in a minute role, can be glimpsed Jimmy Winston, the original keyboards player in The Small Faces. The film was not released until horror specialists AIP bought it and gave it a few UK bookings in late 70 and a belated US showing in early 71. It eventually appeared on TV in 77 – by which time, it had dated rather badly.

The soundtrack was by Pentangle and includes some electronic music from David Vorhaus.

McShane and Gardner

Released December 1970, 106 minutes, colour
DVD: Not available
SOUNDTRACK LP/CD: None released. The 2007 Pentangle CD *The Time Has Come* includes some of the material

CUCUMBER CASTLE

The Bee Gees star and do the music

Talked about from 67 and eventually filmed two years later, by which time The Bee Gees were reduced to the duo of Barry and Maurice Gibb, *Cucumber Castle* was directed by Hugh Gladwish, whose previous credit had been the vapid pop musical *The Ghost Goes Gear*.

The daft plot has the two brothers playing knights in mediaeval England (the King of Cucumber and the King of Jelly) and features an ensemble cast, largely of guest stars, led by Eleanor Bron and Frankie Howerd. After roles in *Help!*, *Bedazzled* and *Women in Love*, this was certainly a change of tack for Bron. The weak comedy script and thin production values are initially puzzling, as if Robert Stigwood couldn't find a better project for his charges, particularly given that his previous venture on TV had been *Cream's Last Concert*. A possible explanation may be that the film was intended by him to replicate for The Bee Gees the huge success that Herman's Hermits and The Monkees had enjoyed in the US with a similar formula: inane dressing-up interspersed with concert footage. Among those glimpsed in *Cucumber Castle* are Blind Faith, Lulu, Roger Daltrey, Donovan, Mick Jagger and Marianne Faithfull, often in shots inserted into the film from other TV and film productions.

A *'Cucumber Castle'* LP (number fifty seven UK/number ninety four US) was released in May 70 containing songs mainly used in the film, including the August 69 hit single *'Don't Forget to Remember'* (number two UK). It would be another seven years, though, before Stigwood and The Bee Gees finally hit box office gold with *Saturday Night Fever*.

BROADCAST: BBC1 26 December 1970, 60 minutes, colour
DVD: Not available
SOUNDTRACK LP/CD: Released on Polydor in May 1970 and reissued on CD 1987

M'mm M'mm Good!

A FRANKOVICH PRODUCTION
PETER SELLERS · GOLDIE HAWN
There's a Girl in My Soup

Screenplay by TERENCE FRISBY based on his original play · Executive Producer JOHN DARK
Produced by M.J. FRANKOVICH and JOHN BOULTING · Directed by ROY BOULTING · COLOR
From Columbia Pictures   **R**   **C**

THERE'S A GIRL IN MY SOUP

Roy Boulting directs
Peter Sellers and Goldie Hawn star

Based on the longest running UK stage comedy of its time, a massive hit about a celebrity chef that was first staged in 66, and subsequently adapted by its author, Terence Frisby, for the big screen, *There's a Girl in My Soup* was efficiently directed by Roy Boulting, and, like the play before it, was a big box office hit. MJ Frankovich co-produced, having just enjoyed huge US successes with the wife swapping comedy *Bob and Carol and Ted and Alice* and the generation gap drama *Cactus Flower*. (In which Walter Matthau fell for… Goldie Hawn, just setting out on her route to stardom after *Rowan and Martin's Laugh-In*.)

Here, Peter Sellers plays a self-centred serial seducer of the opposite sex who duly becomes infatuated with the much younger Goldie Hawn, for whom this was a London based starring vehicle. She eventually outwits him and returns to her rock star boyfriend, Nicky Henson – an actor whose career had actually started several years earlier with a spell as a pop singer on the EMI/Columbia label. The film is well observed, well acted, witty and contains many typical Swinging London trappings.

The soundtrack was produced by Mike d'Abo.

Goldie Hawn and Peter Sellers

Released December 1970, 95 minutes, colour
DVD: Reissued via Sony Pictures Home Entertainment, January 2004
SOUNDTRACK LP/CD: None released

BE GLAD FOR THE SONG HAS NO ENDING

Peter Neal directs
The Incredible String Band star

After significant sales and chart positions for a number of their LPs, The Incredible String Band were clearly, by 70, considered successful enough to front their own TV special, a status previously accorded to The Beatles, The Bee Gees and The Rolling Stones.

The result was this documentary, originally made for the BBC Omnibus Arts series and later given a restricted cinema release. Possibly intended to promote their debut Island LP, released in April 71, it was directed by Peter Neal, who had earned his reputation in folk and rock circles prior to this with *Travelling for a Living*, a 66 BBC documentary about The Watersons and *Experience*, a short about Jimi Hendrix, shot in 68 and released (posthumously) two years later with a narration by Alexis Korner. Joe Boyd produced both the LP and film of this title which consists of two distinct sequences: one where The Incredible String Band perform and talk and the other where they act out a hippyfied costume drama.

No formal soundtrack LP was issued, and the studio release *Be Glad for the Song Has No Ending* did not, alas, enjoy significant sales. Neal would later direct *Glastonbury Fayre* (72) and *Yessongs* (73, released 75).

The Incredible String Band

Released December 1970, 50 minutes, colour
DVD: Released via Music Video Distributor in March 2002
SOUNDTRACK: Released by The Incredible String Band as an LP on Island in April 1971

HURRAY! WE'RE BACHELORS AGAIN

Georg Thomalla and Teri Tordai star

A German comedy produced exclusively for the home market by Rialto, who later backed various Fassbinder films in the 70s and 80s, this stars the hugely popular Georg Thomalla, an actor who dubbed Peter Sellers and Jack Lemmon in German cinema releases of their films and who plays here a not dissimilar type of character. Teri Tordai, an attractive actress in many European horror/sex films (notably the 68 *Tower of Screaming Virgins*), co-stars.

Very much a German entry into the 'straights come to terms with hippies' genre that also spawned *What's Good for the Goose* and *I Love You, Alice B. Toklas*, the plot concerns the marital tribulations and divorces of a middle-aged man and makes an interesting comparison with the Wisdom film.

Mungo Jerry appear in a concert sequence, with other contributions to the soundtrack from German acts The Gloomys and Ricky Shayne. Shayne was a French singer, popular in Germany and Italy, whose early hits were produced by Giorgio Moroder. He appeared in a number of films (including *The Battle of the Mods* 66) and has an acting role here as 'a hippy'.

Georg Thomalla and Terry Tordai

Released January 1971, 90 minutes, colour
DVD: Available on Universum as part of the Georg Thomalla Collection
SOUNDTRACK: None released

PERCY

Ralph Thomas directs
Hywel Bennett stars
The Kinks do the music

Anglo-EMI launched themselves into the film business in the early 70s with a determinedly mainstream roster of productions: cinema versions of TV hits (*Up Pompeii*, *On the Buses*), the Kray brothers-inspired drama *Villain* and this comedy about a man who has a penis transplant… presumably their attempt to compete with the *Carry On* franchise.

Directed by Ralph Thomas, a stalwart of UK features since the 40s who latterly gravitated to the faux Bond spy dramas *Deadlier Than the Male* and *Some Girls Do*, it was based on a novel by Raymond Hitchcock, whose son Robyn would later lead the influential 70s and 80s group The Soft Boys. The script by Hugh Leonard, who mainly did well-upholstered TV adaptations of Dickens and Bronte, contains a great deal of uncredited assistance from Michael Palin. Hywel Bennett stars as the recipient of the new organ who decides to try and trace the donor, and has various adventures en route, particularly with the respectively German and Swedish actresses Elke Sommer and Britt Ekland. The supporting cast was ably led by Denholm Elliott and the film itself, which was X-rated in the UK despite being quite tame, was a huge box office success.

The soundtrack was done by The Kinks and released as an LP in March 71, to no great success, though a single lifted from it, 'God's Children', charted in Australia and New Zealand. In 74, EMI cashed in with a sequel, *Percy's Progress* (aka *It's Not the Size That Counts*) which retained Elliott and Sommer but replaced Bennett with Leigh Lawson and had Judy Geeson, Vincent Price and Julie Ege in a supporting cast that included Harry H Corbett playing the Prime Minister. The plot here is that a catastrophic virus has rendered the entire male population of the planet impotent, except for Percy who has taken up residence on a desert island… reluctantly he returns to do his duty by impregnating enough women to ensure the survival of the human race. Less successful than the original (by 74 there was any number of more explicit sex comedies on offer) it boasted a soundtrack by Tony Macaulay, producer of Edison Lighthouse, Long John Baldry and The Foundations and a theme song from Carl Wayne, formerly lead singer in The Move.

Released March 1971, 103 minutes, colour
DVD: Reissued on Starz/Anchor Bay, December 2001
SOUNDTRACK: Released as an LP by The Kinks on Pye in March 1971. CD reissue on Sanctuary Midline in 2004

GIRL STROKE BOY

Bob Kellett directs
Peter Straker stars

A Hemdale production, and certainly one of the most adventurous films of this era, *Girl Stroke Boy* explores gender confusion, sexual orientation and race issues with a storyline about a vaguely counter-culturish middle class young man who 'after showing no interest in the opposite sex' brings his black and transgender 'girlfriend' home to meet his very conventional suburban parents. A considerable amount of embarrassment and confusion results, most of which is played for laughs.

Directed by Bob Kellett, from a script by Ned Sherrin and Caryl Brahms (both noted contributors to the early 60s satire series *That Was The Week That Was*), the film was based on the David Percival play *Girlfriend* that ran briefly in the West End in 70. It stars Michael Hordern and Joan Greenwood as the parents, Clive Francis (previously seen in the 68 TV adaptation of *Entertaining Mr Sloane*) as the son and singer/actor Peter Straker, from the cast of *Hair*, as the androgynous 'girlfriend'. Like many of the cast of *Hair*, Straker had been signed to a recording deal with Polydor and was an important figure of the time whose later career, which saw him starring in the original production of *The Rocky Horror Show* and recording for RCA, Pye, EMI and Rocket through to the mid 80s, has now been largely forgotten. Ultimately he was better known for his long term relationship with Freddie Mercury; his contribution to promoting a positive image of gay people however remains significant.

Girl Stroke Boy is rarely seen today. A TV screening in the late 70s saw it being classified (wrongly) as an 'adult' film – perhaps an indication of how difficult some people found its subject material. Johnny Scott did the soundtrack – his previous work having included background music in *Help!* and arrangements for Georgie Fame, The Hollies, PJ Proby, Eric Burdon and The Animals and Nirvana.

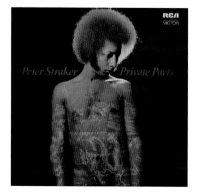

Released 1971, 88 minutes, colour
DVD: Available on Paragon Video
SOUNDTRACK: None released

FRIENDS

Lewis Gilbert directs
Elton John does the music

One of several films made during this period that explored issues to do with the age of consent (of which the massively successful 68 version of *Romeo and Juliet* was the best known with its 15-year-old heroine), *Friends* is a nicely shot poetic romance in which two teenagers (one UK, one French) run away and settle down in a French cottage and have, for a brief period, an idyllic life, including having a child together.

Directed and produced by Lewis Gilbert (a highly regarded figure in UK cinema whose credits ranged from *Reach for The Sky* and *Sink the Bismarck* to *Alfie* and *You Only Live Twice*) it was co-written by him with Vernon Harris – who did the 68 screenplay for *Oliver.* Clearly a serious drama, the leading roles were played by Sean Bury and Anicée Alvina. Bury (sixteen at the time, playing fifteen) made very few other films, but Alvina (seventeen playing fourteen) subsequently enjoyed a significant French career with many other starring roles. The film was critically slated, particularly by Roger Ebert, for its coyness, prurience and cynical marketing of 'youthful innocence' being compared by him to a back edition of the subscription only magazine *Teenage Nudist.* This was quite a put down coming as it did from the man whose own screenplays included the trash epic *Beyond the Valley of the Dolls* and the abortive Sex Pistols vehicle *Who Killed Bambi?* Audiences thought otherwise and the film was sufficiently successful to produce a 74 sequel, *Paul and Michelle.*

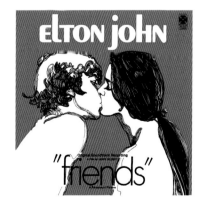

Nominated for a Grammy, the soundtrack was done by Elton John and Bernie Taupin. Then in their first flush of success, it was released as an LP on Paramount and sold well in the US, reaching number thirty six in their LP charts.

Released March 1971, 101 minutes, colour
DVD: Reissued on Paramount in April 1996
SOUNDTRACK: Soundtrack LP released by Elton John on Paramount in April 1971

BREAD

Stanley Long directs
Juicy Lucy star in the music scenes

Made by Stanley Long, the producer of *Groupie Girl* and *This, That and The Other!* (*A Promise of Bed*), this follows a broadly similar commercial format, mixing a young and presumably inexperienced cast with a bit of rock music to produce a rather flimsy film firmly targeted at the burgeoning hippy/youth market. In this instance, though, the grim *News of the World* style moralising approach of *Groupie Girl* is jettisoned for cheerful fun. One contemporary reviewer derided it as '…a Cliff Richard musical with nudes and swearing…' The plot is about a group of friends quitting the Isle of Wight Festival – because it is too commercial – and pitching their tent in a field on their way home, where they decide to hold their own event, with the consent of a friendly local landowner.

A trio of bands duly appear led by the Paul Williams fronted version of Juicy Lucy (whose sax player was, coincidentally, married to the film's screenplay writer, Suzanne Mercer), The Web and Crazy Mabel. The contributions of all three are of a high quality, especially given the analogue vagaries of the time: quirky sound systems, malfunctioning PAs and indifferent mixing. The remainder of the soundtrack was done by John Fiddy, who worked at this time with Uriah Heep on their LP 'Salisbury'.

Released 1971, 79 minutes, colour
DVD: Reissued by the BFI with Permissive in 2009
SOUNDTRACK: None released

MELODY
(S.W.A.L.K.)

Waris Hussein directs
Mark Lester and Jack Wild star in an Alan Parker script

Adolescent misbehaviour in 1971

After their false start with *Connecting Rooms* and difficulties with *Girl Stroke Boy*, Hemdale finally hit their stride with this production. Written by Alan Parker (his first film script after he left advertising) and directed by Waris Hussein – noted for his work on the BBC TV *Wednesday Play* and a film adaptation of the Margaret Drabble novel *A Touch of Love*, that ploughed pretty much the same furrow as *Georgy Girl* – *Melody* starred the *Oliver* partnership of Mark Lester and Jack Wild, supported by 12-year-old model Tracy Hyde.

The rather twee plot, which was filmed in and around Battersea, Kennington and Lambeth, concerns two schoolchildren who announce they are in love and want to get married. The film did not do well in either the UK or the US but was, rather surprisingly, a huge hit in Japan – where the combination of delicate music and images of immaculately groomed diminutive adolescents seems to have struck a chord.

The soundtrack included five tracks written by The Bee Gees, two of which (*In the Morning* and *To Love Somebody*) were standards by this point and the remaining three lifted from their 69 LP *Odessa* (number ten UK/number twenty US). One of these, *Melody Fair*, was released as a single in Japan in April 71, reaching number three in their charts. Also heard in the film are Crosby, Stills, Nash and Young performing *Teach Your Children*. Parker would go on to maintain his interest in mixing film and music with *Bugsy Malone*, *Pink Floyd – The Wall* and *The Commitments*

Released April 1971, 103 minutes, colour
DVD: Reissued by Optimum Home Releasing, March 2010
SOUNDTRACK: Released as an LP on Polydor in Germany in 1971

NOT TONIGHT, DARLING

Anthony Sloman directs
Thunderclap Newman do the music

If Marianne Faithfull and Jane Birkin blazed the trail for mixing music with acting, they were run a close second during this period by the now largely forgotten Luan Peters. A trouper of the UK scene, almost in the manner of the earlier generation of variety artistes, she recorded as Karol Keyes for EMI/Columbia and Fontana from 64 (including a very capable April 66 cover of the Ike and Tina Turner hit 'A Fool in Love') whilst touring up and down the country and taking minor TV and stage roles. After a false start with *Go Girl*, a thirteen part series about the adventures of a jet-setting crime fighting go-go dancer (which was made but never broadcast), she signed to Polydor and landed the lead role in *Not Tonight, Darling*, one of seven films she would make in the early 70s.

A not untypical UK second feature (albeit one in which Fiona Richmond can be spotted in a minute role), it was directed by film editor Anthony Sloman who, after one further offering, *Foursome/Sweet and Sexy* (72), returned to his former occupation. The plot, a predictable framework around which various sexual adventures could be built, concerns a housewife who has an affair with a door-to-door salesman; she is being spied on by a peeping tom and gets her revenge on him and on the person who put him up to it. A modest success, Peters continued to mix acting with singing, scoring a big hit in 75 with disco act 5000 Volts, before fading into obscurity.

An appearance is made by Thunderclap Newman, performing three songs from their LP *'Hollywood Dream'* in a sequence set in a club. Recollecting this many years later, Andy 'Thunderclap' Newman remembered they were given to understand that the film 'was something like James Bond' and were told to just play their material whilst the actors and crew shot scenes in the background. The soundtrack was done by Denis King, previously one of the 50s-60s pop act The King Brothers, and brother-in-law of actress Carol White.

Released 1971, 90 minutes, colour
DVD: Reissued by Music Video Distributors In May 2007
SOUNDTRACK: None released

EXTREMES

Tony Klinger directs
Supertramp star in the music section

Produced by Barry Jacobs (whose other credits include *Groupie* and *Bread*), this was directed and written by Tony Klinger, a mere twenty-one at the time, whose access to the upper reaches of the film industry owed more than a little to his father being the producer of *Get Carter*.

Extremes is a documentary about the life of counter-culture young people in London, featuring Hells Angels, hippies, pop fans, drug addicts and assorted members of the 'alternative society'. It examines the various strands that youth culture had separated into by the early 70s and was publicised on its release by the *International Times*, being sufficiently well made to avoid being categorised as an exploitative cash-in. Among the footage are some lengthy sequences filmed at the 70 Isle of Wight Festival. Klinger would maintain his interest in music and later produced *The Kids Are Alright*, an influential 1979 documentary about The Who that gave rise to a brief revival in mod culture.

The soundtrack was delegated to Roger Cook, better known as one half of David and Jonathan (see *Modesty Blaise*) and a writer of pleasant commercial hits for The Fortunes, Gene Pitney, Whistling Jack Smith, Blue Mink and White Plains. This, though, is strictly greatcoat and flares territory with contributions from Supertramp, Arc and Crucible (which turned out to be a pseudonym used by White Plains). An LP of the film's music appeared on Deram in 72.

Released 1971, 82 minutes, colour
DVD: None available
SOUNDTRACK: LP issued on Deram in 1972

UNIVERSAL SOLDIER

Cy Endfield directs
George Lazenby stars
Phillip Goodhand-Tait does the music

London 1970. A disillusioned rock star, with a penchant for sexual threesomes, falls out with his gangster-like manager and promptly dies in a drug and alcohol induced haze in Notting Hill: an accurate description of the last days of Jimi Hendrix who, in an instance of life imitating art, in this case the film *Performance*, died just before he was (according to some) about to begin filming *Universal Soldier*.

The second feature from Radio Caroline entrepreneur Ronan O'Rahilly, *Universal Soldier* had a long, somewhat shambolic, gestation. Trailed as a major counter-culture event (with its making and release covered in *International Times*), O'Rahilly benefitted from being the manager of George Lazenby, the then James Bond, whom he advised to abandon the 007 franchise in favour of this film about a world-weary mercenary from post-colonial Africa coming to terms with the modern world and finally seeing the benefits of a chilled-out hippy lifestyle.

Germaine Greer

It appeared, on paper, to have everything going for it. Donald Factor, who had just produced the early Robert Altman film *That Cold Day in the Park*, agreed to part fund the project and Cy Endfield – noted for his tremendous UK success *Zulu* and whose previous film had been a psychedelic version of *De Sade* with a soundtrack from Sinatra and Presley collaborator Billy Strange – would direct. Tony Imi, who had shot *Cathy Come Home* and *The Body* was cameraman, the script was a collaborative effort mainly involving Joe Massot (who had directed *Wonderwall* and was about to do the hippy western *Zachariah*) and Derek Marlowe (author of *A Dandy in Aspic*). Lazenby was the latest man to play 007, and therefore a star, and the highest placed female role in the cast was taken by Germaine Greer... just catapulting to worldwide fame at this point as the radical feminist author of *The Female Eunuch*. Even the death of Hendrix didn't seem that crucial: he was replaced as co-star by Ben Carruthers, a major figure in US independent/experimental cinema (in Cassavetes' *Shadows*, with Ginsberg in *Guns of the Trees*), who had relocated to Europe in 65 where he promptly recorded, as Ben Carruthers and The Deep, a highly collectable single, 'Jack O' Diamonds', released on EMI/Parlophone, on which he was backed by Jimmy Page and Nicky Hopkins among others.

But there were two problems – money and drugs. O'Rahilly seems to have got funding from wherever he could but there was never quite enough to produce a properly made film. Re drugs, Lazenby recollected, some years later, that the script was rarely adhered to as the cast generally improvised after consumption of considerable amounts of cannabis. The end result, with its muffled soundtrack and lack of crisp editing, could have been so much better with just slightly more care. Shot in a tired, dingy-looking, end-of-the-decade London, with many scenes occurring in and around Portobello Road, together with an almost obligatory scene in the Bunny Club, the film has a certain doomed *fin de siècle* quality.

The soundtrack was delegated to Rodger Bain, then producing Black Sabbath, whose initial releases – in what was then a conventional 'progressive' hard rock/blues rock style – enjoyed considerable success in both the US and the UK. He passed on much of the work to Phillip Goodhand-Tait, an elegiac singer-songwriter of the type then in vogue. Featuring fifteen pieces of music, recorded over two days in May 71, it includes his own version of 'One Road' (a hit he wrote for The Love Affair in early 69) as well as material from his LP 'I Think I'll Write a Song'.

Previewed in bits at the NFT, *Universal Soldier* flopped on release in late 71 and eventually crept out in the US as a supporting feature to the AIP biker film, *The Dirt Gang*. Lazenby sacked O'Rahilly and Goodhand-Tait's soundtrack was denied an official release.

Released 1971, 96 minutes, colour
DVD: No release – VHS video version released in mid 80s
SOUNDTRACK LP/CD: No release

Phun City
THE BEST CONCERT FILM YOU'LL NEVER SEE?

Intended as a fund raiser for *International Times*, the premier underground paper in the UK, the Phun City Festival, held in Sussex in July 70, was organised by Ronan O'Rahilly, then something of a popular hero after his activities with Radio Caroline and his *succès d'estime* with *The Girl on a Motorcycle*. Claiming that he only had sufficient finance to pay for some site security and a PA system, and insisting that the bands and poets due to appear performed for free, O'Rahilly announced that his company, Mid Atlantic Films, then working on *Universal Soldier*, the George Lazenby follow-up to *On Her Majesty's Secret Service*, would film the entire event, thus producing something to equal *Monterey Pop* or *Woodstock* in its scope and portrayal of the cultural proclivities of contemporary UK youth.

Proceeding in typically English weather over three days (the *International Times* had wanted seven), the music was terrific with blistering performances from, among others, The Pretty Things, Mighty Baby, Pink Fairies (who appeared nude), The Edgar Broughton Band, a UK debut from US politico-rockers MC5, Michael Chapman, Sonja Kristina (from the cast of *Hair*), and Mungo Jerry. By all accounts, the poetry – delivered by Pete Brown and William Burroughs – wasn't bad either.

Alas... for reasons that are not clear, Phun City lost £6,000 (the equivalent of £150,000 today) and provided no funds for the *International Times*. O'Rahilly never produced a film of the event for public release and the extensive amounts of supposedly excellent footage that were shot and seen by some of the participants are now considered lost: only a scattering of colour stills remains to record the event. Whilst the Dutch managed to make *Love and Music* and the French *Guitare au poing* (both films of festivals that took place in 70), the UK had to wait until *Glastonbury Fayre* (72) for an indigenous release.

BEWARE OF
A HOLY WHORE

Rainer Werner Fassbinder directs
Eddie Constantine and Hanna Schygulla star

Considered by Rainer Werner Fassbinder to be the best of the thirty nine films he directed in a sixteen year career, *Beware of a Holy Whore* was shot back-to-back by him with an arty western, *Whity*, in Spain in 70-71.The plot has a group of disparate actors and actresses marooned in a hotel in Spain, idling their time away whilst they wait for the arrival of the director and star to start shooting a film: very much as happened in real life to the cast and crew of both films.

The leading roles were played by Eddie Constantine, whose prior credits included Godard's *Alphaville* and Lou Castel, previously seen in the spaghetti western *A Bullet for the General* and the Italian trash thriller *Paranoia/Orgasmo*. Marquard Bohm, who had appeared in the German sci-fi thriller *A Big Grey-Blue Bird/Ein grosser graublauer Vogel* (which had a score by Can), co-stars with Fassbinder regular Hanna Schygulla. The end result is visually attractive, funny and contains a wealth of early 70s decor.

The soundtrack was supervised by Peer Raben and includes contributions from Spooky Tooth, taken from their 69 LP *'Spooky Two'*, and Leonard Cohen, which are heard in the film being played on a jukebox by the cast.

Lou Castel and Hanna Schygulla

Released September 1971, 103 minutes, colour
DVD: Reissued by Well Spring in 2003
SOUNDTRACK: Reissued in Germany on a CD by Alhambra

How HAIR! Made
Oscar a Star...

The two way traffic between UK pop and film during the 60s and early 70s produced several troubadours who both acted and sang – Murray Head immediately comes to mind – but arguably the most successful to emerge was Paul Nicholas, who made the transition from the normally staid world of West End theatre to major cinema roles in 70. Prior to this, he was one of the troupers of the UK pop scene... playing piano for a couple of years with Screaming Lord Sutch, an English cardboard, end-of-the-pier version of Screamin' Jay Hawkins, before trying his luck, as Oscar, with straight mod material (*'Join My Gang'* – Pete Townshend) and comic Anthony Newley mannerisms (*'Over the Wall We Go'* – David Bowie). Luckily, he was managed by Robert Stigwood, who cast him in the musical *Hair* which premiered in London in September 68 after nearly a year of success in New York.

Like the US west coast flower power phenomenon on which it was based, this was an import that illustrated how much the recently

attained British hegemony in music and culture was slipping away and London was no longer the automatic capital of the pop world. Still, it was a box office smash and the frisson of excitement caused by the cast appearing nude (for twenty seconds) immediately propelled two female members of the company to stardom: Marsha Hunt, who almost became Mrs Jagger, wowed the Isle of Wight Festival, cut the brilliant LP *'Woman Child'*, returned to the West End in *Catch My Soul* (with PJ Proby and PP Arnold) and appeared in *Dracula AD 1972*; and Sonja Kristina, lead singer of Curved Air, one of the better British bands of the time, fondly remembered for their 71 hit *'Back Street Luv'* and a trio of big selling albums. The London cast recording of *Hair*, released as an LP on Polydor in December 68, confirmed the magnitude of this event – reaching number three, remaining in the charts until September 70 and even denting the US Hot 100. It easily outsold every UK film soundtrack of the era.

Now an established act, Nicholas moved quickly into films with co-starring roles in *Cannabis (French Intrigue)* (70) and *What Became of Jack and Jill?* (71) before returning to the stage to play *Jesus Christ Superstar* (another Stigwood show) alongside Dana Gillespie. Latterly in such 70s excesses as *Lisztomania* (75) and *Sgt. Pepper's*

Marsha Hunt   *Sonja Kristina*

Lonely Hearts Club Band (78), it's interesting that both he and *Hair* co-star Oliver Tobias finished the decade starring in potboilers like *The World Is Full of Married Men* and *The Stud*.

A tendency towards flashiness and outré behaviour was the common denominator for many associated with *Hair*. The backing band was led by Alex Harvey, later a colourful and highly theatrical figure in pre-punk UK rock, whilst bit part players Richard O'Brien and Tim Curry devised and starred in the global smash *The Rocky Horror Show*, now one of the longest running franchises in stage history. It is interesting to speculate what an original UK pop musical of the period would have looked like. The closest candidate, Pete Townshend's *Tommy*, was performed three times in public in 72-73 with a cast that included, at various points, Peter Sellers, Ringo Starr, Steve Winwood, Roy Wood, Marsha Hunt, Rod Stewart, David Essex and Elkie Brooks. Curiously, though, no attempt was made – at that point – to stage it as a major theatrical production.

Rick Wakeman as Siegfried (left) and Paul Nicholas as Wagner in Ken Russell's Lisztomania (1975)

PRIVATE ROAD

Barney Platts-Mills director
Bruce Robinson and Susan Penhaligon star

Susan Penhaligon

Before making his reputation with the screenplay for *The Killing Fields* (84) and directing the fag-end-of-the-60s hippy drama *Withnail and I* (87), Bruce Robinson had acting ambitions. In 68 he co-starred in *The Other People*, with Peter McEnery, which, despite its heavyweight credits (produced by Michael Deeley who also did *The Knack* and *The Italian Job*, soundtrack by Johnny Dankworth), has never been released and, in 71, he had top billing in *Private Road*, a semi-improvised exploration charting the end of 60s idealism and the second film directed by Barney Platts-Mills.

The plot centres on a young middle class woman (Susan Penhaligon) who attempts to escape her ultra-suburban respectable family via a relationship with a struggling writer (Bruce Robinson). They relocate to the wilds of Scotland but, eventually, he ends up working in advertising.

The cast includes Michael Feast, from the London production of *Hair*, and Catherine Howe, a highly rated and collectable acid folk artist of the period, in an acting role. The film, which from its general tone does not suggest that UK society has a particularly optimistic future, won a prize at the Locarno Film Festival.

The soundtrack was assembled by David Dundas who, later in the decade, would release the chart hit '*Jeans On*'.

Released September 1971, 89 minutes, colour
DVD: Reissued by the BFI in January 2011
SOUNDTRACK: None issued

Hammer
THE POP YEARS

With British cinemas awash, by the late 60s, with US and European films that set new standards in graphic violence and sexuality, Hammer, with its carefully presented reworkings of nineteenth century chestnuts like *Frankenstein* and *Dracula*, filmed in a country house near London with interchangeable repertory company casts, suddenly looked very old hat by comparison.

To keep up with changes in public taste, the studio duly ventured into space drama with *Moon Zero Two* (69) and recruited a few new faces. Prominent among these was Tudor Gates, whose prior screenplay credits included *Dateline Diamonds* (65), *Danger: Diabolik* (67), *Better a Widow* and *Barbarella* (both 68) – all of which suggested he might be the person to reboot the studio. At Hammer, Gates turned out *The*

Vampire Lovers (70 – a co-production with AIP which made *The Haunted House of Horror* and *Scream and Scream Again*), *Lust for a Vampire* (71), with Radio One DJ Mike Raven in a supporting role, and *Twins of Evil* (72) co-starring the *Playboy* centrefolds the Collinson sisters, and with folk singers the Chanter Sisters in uncredited minor roles. All were modest successes. Elsewhere, Hammer added jazz to *Crescendo* (70 – soundtrack by Malcolm Williamson) and *Straight on Till Morning* (72 – title song by Annie Ross), and really pushed the boat out with *Demons of the Mind* (72) which featured Gillian Hills and Paul Jones.

For whatever reasons, though… the endemic lack of funds in the UK film industry… English reserve… the studio just couldn't compete effectively with the huge number of more explicit, sophisticated and, frankly, better horror and suspense films exemplified by the *giallo* genre. Their main star, Christopher Lee, quit in search of better material after *Dracula AD 1972* (he later made *Death Line* and *The Wicker Man* elsewhere), and, after a couple of Kung Fu collaborations with Hong Kong veteran Run Run Shaw in the mid 70s, Hammer pulled out of film to concentrate on TV and then ceased production completely. Fondly remembered, as is the *Carry On* series (which had its heyday at the same time) and even relaunched in 2010, it is worth pointing out that, between 71 and 74, Hammer produced twenty six films. During the same period, Jesus Franco (of *Paroxismus/ Venus in Furs* and much else) alone directed thirty two and Franco was merely one of many French, German, Italian, Spanish and US directors working in the same field.

THE TRAGEDY OF MACBETH

Roman Polanski directs
Jon Finch stars
The Third Ear Band do the music

A project initiated by Roman Polanski after the August 69 murder of his partner, Sharon Tate, and seen therefore as a cathartic experience for him, *The Tragedy of Macbeth* (perhaps not surprisingly) struggled to get Hollywood backing, despite boasting a screenplay by Kenneth Tynan. The production eventually moved to the UK after Victor Lownes arranged funding via Hugh Hefner's Playboy Productions, with Andrew Braunsberg (who had previously done *Wonderwall*) co-producing. Tynan and Hefner had previously collaborated on the US sex film *Freedom to Love* (69) which extolled the virtues of complete, consensual liberalism.

Filmed on locations in Snowdonia National Park and at Bamburgh Castle, Northumberland, the film had a young, attractive cast and starred Jon Finch (a major selling point after his appearance in *Sunday Bloody Sunday*), Francesca Annis and Martin Shaw. It subsequently emerged that Hefner expected all the actresses to be available for *Playboy* centerfolds (they declined). A conspicuous amount of onscreen nudity – no doubt influenced by this – and graphic violence do occur but it is generally reckoned a good version of the play.

A soundtrack of eerie music was provided by the Third Ear Band.

Released October 1971, 140 minutes, colour
DVD: Reissued by Sony Pictures Home Entertainment in May 2002
SOUNDTRACK: Issued as the LP '*Music from Macbeth*' by the Third Ear Band on EMI/Harvest in 1972. Reissued as a CD by BGO in 1990

LOVE AND MUSIC
(STAMPING GROUND)

George Sluizer and Hans Pohland direct
Pink Floyd star in the music scenes

After the huge success of *Monterey Pop*, the race was on for a similar film of a European event: the UK had *Phun City*, France, *Guitare au poing* and the Netherlands, *Love and Music* – an extended concert movie showcasing the Holland Pop Festival, staged at Kralingen, just outside Rotterdam, in June 70, and billed as the 'European Woodstock'.

Directed by George Sluizer and Hans Pohland, Sluizer's background in National Geographic documentaries is apparent from much of the footage. Crowds of hippies gathering and camping in a field, discarding their clothes, taking drugs and giving rather stoned interviews, all being recorded in a style akin to an expedition filming Amazonian Indians. Prior to cooperating on this, his colleague Pohland had directed *Auf Scheisser schiess man nicht* (69), with a soundtrack by Edgar Froese of Tangerine Dream, and had just returned from Nigeria where he had made an adaptation of Chinua Achebe's classic novel of African decolonisation *Things Fall Apart*.

The music is terrific, with a huge variety of acts appearing, including from the UK alone: Al Stewart, Quintessence, T. Rex, Pink Floyd, East of Eden, Family and The Soft Machine. The concert sequences are, in fact, very well done - the editor on the film was Roger Spottiswoode, who would rise to fame some years later as the writer of *48 Hrs* and the director of a series of blockbusters through the 80s and 90s.

Released October 1971, 83 minutes, colour
DVD: Reissued as a double bill with *Glastonbury Fayre* by Odeon Entertainment in June 2009. Also available separately on a Brazilian only DVD release.
SOUNDTRACK: None released

A CLOCKWORK ORANGE

Stanley Kubrick directs
Malcolm McDowell stars

Stanley Kubrick's follow up to his massive global success with *2001: A Space Odyssey* was his adaptation of the 62 Anthony Burgess novel *A Clockwork Orange* that explores pointless violence, urban gangs and general delinquency and how different political versions of the state – whether politically left or right – deal with these. What emerges is a bitterly dystopian vision, filmed over seven months in 70 and 71, with much of the footage shot on the newly built Thamesmead Estate, near Woolwich.

It stars Malcolm McDowell, then enjoying considerable box office clout following his 68 success in *If...*, as the key and very violent protagonist. Explicitly sexual in parts, the strong supporting cast includes actress and singer Gillian Hills – as one of two girls (ten years old in the book, fourteen here) picked up by McDowell in a record shop for an extended bout of

The Droogs looking for trouble on Thamesmead Estate

threeway sex. Curiously, she was seen previously in similar circumstances with Jane Birkin and David Hemmings in *Blow-Up*. After the huge success enjoyed by the soundtrack LP for Kubrick's previous effort *2001: A Space Odyssey* (number three UK, number twenty four US and a three year chart run), it was fully expected that *A Clockwork Orange* would replicate this. What emerged was broadly similar: a mixture of classical pieces, some reworked on synthesisers by Walter Carlos… who rather confusingly underwent gender reassignment during the recording and mixing, to emerge as Wendy Carlos. In addition, Kubrick wanted to include segments from Pink Floyd's 'Atom Heart Mother', reserving the right to cut and edit the music to the screen action. Roger Waters refused, so Kubrick turned instead to the psychedelic folk group Sunforest and used two of their compositions on the official soundtrack release. The notoriety generated by *A Clockwork Orange* on its release resulted in huge sales for the accompanying soundtrack LP - arguably making it, apart from *Help!*, *Yellow Submarine* and *Let It Be*, the biggest selling example of a rock/pop influenced soundtrack during this period, with chart positions of number four UK and number thirty four US and an eleven month chart run. It was released with a short supporting animated film by Bob Godfrey (who had drawn some of the episodes in the 65-67 US cartoon series *The Beatles*) – *Kama Sutra Rides Again* – in which a desperately suburban couple experiment with sexual positions.

A tremendous UK box office success, the film certainly polarised public opinion, being withdrawn from circulation by Kubrick after it began being blamed (falsely) by the UK media for encouraging copycat crimes, with the result that his own house and family were besieged by crowds of protesting demonstrators. Unable to be viewed in the UK for many years – except via bootleg copies – an unauthorised screening of it in 93 caused the closure of the Scala Cinema.

Released December 1971, 137 minutes, colour
DVD: Reissued by Warner Home Video September 2001
SOUNDTRACK: Released as an LP by Wendy Carlos by Columbia in 1972

FATA MORGANA

Werner Herzog directs
The Sahara Desert stars

FATA MORGANA

With no conventional plot (it's allegorical…), an unknown cast, part vaguely anti-colonial documentary and part road movie – not a genre that UK film makers ever really pursued – *Fata Morgana* is a good example of the type of feature screened in student union film societies and the burgeoning number of small independent cinemas in the early and mid 70s, usually as a late night show, with plenty of wine and smoking material to hand.

Made by Werner Herzog immediately before he hit his stride with *Aguirre – Wrath of God*, *Fata Morgana* was shot on location in and around the Sahara Desert and contains images of mirages… hence its title (a *fata morgana* is an unusual and complex form of mirage)… and a narration about creation myths. Its slow tracking shots of shabby colonial buildings, wrecked and abandoned western technology and similar was noted by *Time Out* magazine, which considered it to be, on its release, '…the nearest thing yet to a genuine political science fiction movie…'

The film is punctuated with suitably trippy musical contributions from the Third Ear Band, Blind Faith, John Renbourn and Leonard Cohen. Cohen was on something of a roll at this point, with his material also being used in *Beware of a Holy Whore* and the Robert Altman western *McCabe and Mrs Miller.*

Released October 1971, 79 minutes, colour
DVD: Reissued as part of the Werner Herzog Collection, August 2005
SOUNDTRACK: None released

PERMISSIVE

Lindsay Shonteff directs
Simon Napier-Bell does the music

A cheaply made b-movie, written by Jeremy Craig Dryden (who had previously done *Run with the Wind*, a 66 beatnik drama with Shawn Phillips and Francesca Annis), about a provincial girl arriving in London and becoming a groupie, this was directed by Lindsay Shonteff, whose credits in the 60s and 70s include many exploitation films across several different genres.

Filmed in drab London settings, with almost everything looking bleak and unsatisfactory, it has Maggie Stride and Gilbert Wynne in the lead roles at the head of a rather minor and inexpensive cast. In fact, the film can be seen today as more an illustration of the dingy life lived by marginal pop and rock acts at the time than as an interesting moral panic drama. Forever More, who released two LPs on RCA and who were managed by Simon Napier-Bell (previously in charge, at various times, of The Yardbirds and John's Children), both act and perform here having already gone through several changes by this point. As the Scotch of St James, they had left the Scottish ballroom circuit for the bright lights of London in 66, evolving within a few years into Hopscotch (in which guise they made a contribution to the film *If It's Tuesday, This Must Be Belgium*). Their line-up included Mick Travis, once in Band of Joy with Robert Plant and John Bonham. In an intriguing 'what if' footnote in rock history, Travis had been held in reserve, with Ian Hunter, for a couple of months in 68 by Mickie Most as a possible member of The New Yardbirds, should Peter Grant's rival attempts to form a viable ensemble not succeed. (They did and became Led Zeppelin.) *Permissive*, filmed in 70 and released eighteen months later, did not make stars of Forever More whose two main members, Alan Gorrie and Onnie McIntyre, drifted back to Scotland after doing two more quick scores for Lindsay Shonteff, *The Yes Girls* (71) and *The Fast Kill* (72). They returned a few years later as the driving force in the Average White Band, to immense worldwide acclaim.

The film soundtrack includes contributions from Titus Groan and Comus, both 'progressive' acts signed to the Pye Records 'progressive' subsidiary Dawn

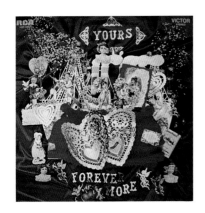

Released February 1972, 90 minutes,
colour
DVD: Reissued as part of the BFI
Flipside series in January 2010
SOUNDTRACK: None released

CHRISTA
(SWEDISH FLY GIRLS)

Jack O'Connell directs
Manfred Mann does the music

Birte Tove

After writing, directing and producing the 68 US documentary *Revolution*, with Quicksilver Messenger Service and Country Joe and the Fish, Jack O'Connell headed to Europe and, in particular, Scandinavia – noted for its liberal censorship – to make *Christa*, his first feature and a film produced by Mogens Skot-Hansen, whose next venture was *King Lear*, with Paul Scofield and Benni Korzen, who, many years later, would oversee *Babette's Feast*.

Premiered at Cannes in 71, with an original running time of almost four hours, this was a relatively serious drama, albeit one with a significant amount of nudity and sex, that was eventually cut by more than fifty per cent and renamed *Swedish Fly Girls* for its UK and US cinema release, several months later. The plot, set mainly in Copenhagen, is about an air hostess (whose uniform – a fetishist's dream – appears to be made of UPV) who is separated from her husband and child and has various affairs in the course of her work. The cast was international: Birte Tove starred with Clinton Greyn (whose other credits included *Robbery* (67) and the TV spy series *Virgin of the Secret Service* (68) and Daniel Gélin, also seen in the Birkin-Gainsbourg film *Slogan*, in support. It is said that it went on to gross $60m worldwide.

The soundtrack was originally written by Al Kooper, whose material (written after his exit from Blood, Sweat and Tears) was not used. Instead, the film score was arranged and recorded by Manfred Mann, with the rhythm section from the London stage production of *Hair*, in the spring and summer of 70, and includes a number of songs written by O'Connell and Mose Henry (latter formerly of US folk act The Highwaymen) who also perform some of these. Other material is sung by Sandy Denny and Melanie. The arrangements and incidental music were by Derek Wadsworth, who otherwise worked with Christine Perfect/McVie and Dusty Springfield.

Released 1972, 100 minutes, colour
DVD: Status of current release unclear
SOUNDTRACK: LP released on Juno in 1972

Jack Findlay gets a hand

CONTINENTAL CIRCUS

Jérôme Laperrousaz directs
Gong do the music

A documentary feature about motorcycle racers, made using footage from various events in the late 60s, this includes a great deal of material showing Jack Findlay, an Australian who won the French Grand Prix in 63 and was the leading rider of the time.

Directed by Jérôme Laperrousaz, who had previously made the concert movie *Amougies*, the film took its name from the 'Continental Circus' – a description of the riders who moved nomadically from one race to another, usually by van/caravan, whilst scraping a living from the money paid by the race organisers, negotiating with the business end of the sport and remaining independent. An analogy of sorts is thus made with the crowds of hippies who trekked from music festival to music festival at the same time.

Produced by Filmanthrope who later did the anarchic sex comedy *Themroc* (73), in which the cast speak gibberish, the soundtrack was by Daevid Allen and Gong and subsequently appeared as an LP by them on Philips. Laperoussaz remained active, his next film being the 75 sci-fi drama *Hu-man*, with Terence Stamp.

Released July 1972, 102 minutes, colour
DVD: Current status unclear
SOUNDTRACK: LP released on Byg Records in January 1971

FOUR DIMENSIONS OF GRETA

Pete Walker directs
Harry South does the music

This is the second film made by Pete Walker, who directed many not dissimilar sex or horror films, from a screenplay by Murray Smith. This followed their earlier collaboration, *Cool it Carol* (70), which had starred Robin Askwith, a huge star of 70s UK sex comedies, with pre-Beatles pop star Jess Conrad in a major supporting role. Here, Tristan Rogers and Karen Boyes head a cast that also features Askwith, and, in a minor part as 'balding hippy', Richard O'Brien who, like Paul Nicholas (*Cannabis*), Michael Heap (*Private Road*) and Peter Straker (*Girl Stroke Boy*), was a veteran of the London stage production of *Hair*.

The plot is about a private detective who is hired by a wealthy German family to search for their daughter, who has become enmeshed in the lurid world of Soho and its attendant… a narrative that therefore allows for a thorough exploration of various establishments, their owners, performers and clientele.

The soundtrack was done by Harry South, one of the mainstays of the UK jazz scene from the early 50s, and leader for many years of the premier UK big band. His other musical exploits during this period included the 'Sound Venture' LP with Georgie Fame (a number nine hit in the UK album charts in 66) and the theme for *The Sweeney* TV series.

Released May 1972, 90 minutes, colour
DVD: Reissued by Salvation in November 2000
SOUNDTRACK: None released

GLASTONBURY FAYRE

Peter Neal directs
David Puttnam produces

With no fewer than four producers, of whom three (Si Litvinoff, Sanford Lieberson and David Puttnam) would rank as major figures in cinema, and directed by Peter Neal (who had previously done *Be Glad for the Song Has No Ending*) assisted by Nicolas Roeg… this is the concert documentary of the 71 Glastonbury Festival. The first major British concert film to get anywhere near a wide cinema release (which rather demonstrates how much the UK trailed the US, France and the Netherlands by 71-72), it shows the event long before it became a major family occasion with a mere 10,000 or so souls in attendance.

Glastonbury had in fact first been held in 1970, when a crowd of only 1500 watched T Rex, Quintessence, Al Stewart, Keith Christmas, Stackridge, Amazing Blondel and Sam Apple Pie: an event captured in the 70 TV documentary *London Rock*. Here, a year later the bill was expanded to feature Melanie, The Edgar Broughton Band, Quintessence (again), The Pink Fairies, Terry Reid, Gong, David Bowie, Hawkwind, Arthur Brown's Kingdom Come, Family, Brinsley Schwarz, Fairport Convention, Traffic and Mighty Baby. These perform whilst the counter-culture is seen against all the usual backdrops: naked dancing, camp fires, crowds arriving and departing, vans and buses covered in improvised artwork etc.

The soundtrack (now a highly collectable triple LP) was released in April 72 and contains material by Brinsley Schwarz, Mighty Baby, David Bowie, Skin Alley, The Pink Fairies, The Edgar Broughton Band, Gong, Hawkwind, The Grateful Dead, Marc Bolan and Pete Townshend – not all of whom actually played at the Festival.

Released May 1972, 87 minutes, colour
DVD: Reissued by Odeon Entertainment in June 2009
SOUNDTRACK: Originally released on Revelation Records in April 1972. Reissued October 2006

LA VALLÉE
(OBSCURED BY CLOUDS)

Barbet Schroeder directs
Pink Floyd do the music

Filmed on location in Papua New Guinea, at a time when 60s utopianism was in retreat in the US and UK, this was written and directed by Barbet Schroeder as his follow-up to *More* and concerns young European travellers who head into a remote area and, among other things, have an encounter with indigenous people.

Well made, and with excellent photography, it stars Michael Gothard, previously seen in supporting roles in *Scream and Scream Again* and *The Devils*, and Jean-Pierre Kalfon, whose credits included Jean-Luc Godard's *Weekend*, the psychedelic pop musical *Les Idoles* and a co-starring role with Jacques Brel in *Bonnot's Gang*. The film was popular for many years after its release with independent cinemas and student audiences.

The dreamy soundtrack was composed by Pink Floyd and released as an LP. It enjoyed heavy sales, reaching number one in France, number four in the Netherlands, number six in the UK and number forty six in the US. Schroeder had a long career in high quality French cinema and later directed *Barfly* (87), an adaptation of an autobiographical work by LA dropout Charles Bukowski, with Mickey Rourke and Faye Dunaway.

Released June 1972, 106 minutes, colour
DVD: Reissued on Homevision in February 2003
SOUNDTRACK: LP originally released – as *Obscured by Clouds* – on Harvest by Pink Floyd in June 1972. CD reissue on EMI in 1995

GOLD

Ronan O'Rahilly produces
MC5 do the music

The MC5

An independent US film, originally shot in 68-69 by a community theatre project run by Bill Desloge and Bob Levis, this was taken over and completed by pirate radio entrepreneur Ronan O'Rahilly some years later, after Desloge and Levis had approached him (in the wake of the success of *The Girl on a Motorcycle*) and suggested a collaborative venture.

Basically an improvised hippy farce about the discovery of gold in a small town and the effect this has on the inhabitants, its shambolic plot features much sex and nudity. In the minor US cast can be spotted noted musician Dan Hicks, previously of The Charlatans and later of Dan Hicks and his Hot Licks.

The soundtrack is better than the film and includes music by electronic composer Warner Jepson. O'Rahilly brought MC5 back to the UK in early 72 to record specifically for the film – the material yielded from this being the last they produced before breaking-up. David McWilliams and Barry St John, both artists on the Major Minor label (owned by the major financial backers of Radio Caroline) can also be heard in the film.

Like O'Rahilly's other venture *Universal Soldier*, it flopped at the box office, being released for a couple of weeks in a small sex cinema in Soho in late 72. It was quickly forgotten but subsequently resurfaced to moderate acclaim as an interesting time capsule of its era.

Released August 1972, 89 minutes, colour
DVD: Reissued by Bob Levis Productions in 2009 (contact: levis4402@yahoo.com)
SOUNDTRACK: No official release

MADE

Joseph Janni produces
Carol White and Roy Harper star

Howard Barker was twenty four years old when his play *No One Was Saved* became the latest hit to emanate from the Royal Court Theatre. Taking its title and plot from The Beatles song *'Eleanor Rigby'*, it sets out a grim story about a single parent (based on Eleanor), her tribulations with various men, including a folk/rock musician (based on/inspired by John Lennon) and her attempts to find a way out of her situation.

A film version quickly followed. Produced by Joseph Janni, one of the most significant figures at that time in the UK film industry, whose work had included *A Kind of Loving*, *Billy Liar*, *Modesty Blaise*, *Poor Cow* and *Sunday Bloody Sunday*, it was directed by John Mackenzie, who had just finished *Unman, Wittering and Zigo*, another film adaptation of a then notable play, with David Hemmings. The leading roles were taken by Carol White and Roy Harper, the latter cast after Kris Kristofferson, Marc Bolan and Tony Joe White had turned the part down. The end result, filmed in particularly grimy parts of Woolwich in south east London, was one of the better and more realistic dramas to appear in UK cinemas in the early 70s – and very much the opposite of the utopian optimism that had epitomised The Beatles' impact on film and music only a short time earlier.

Roy Harper and Carol White

Harper also did the songs for the soundtrack, a number of which appear on his 73 LP *'Lifemask'*. Harper never made another acting appearance and Barker quit cinema after adapting *Aces High* (76) with Malcolm McDowell. John Mackenzie eventually made his reputation with *The Long Good Friday* (80), a classy British crime thriller and, not unlike *Made*, an exploration of the bleak environment of inner London at that time.

Released August 1972, 101 minutes, colour
DVD: Not currently available
SOUNDTRACK: No release

THE ALF GARNETT SAGA

Bob Kellett directs
Warren Mitchell stars

Warren Mitchell dreams of Julie Ege

With UK feature film starts hitting new lows throughout the early 70s, producers, noting the huge 69 success of *Till Death Us Do Part*, eagerly switched to big screen versions of TV comedies and dramas. EMI, in particular, blazed the trail, turning out *Up Pompeii*, *On the Buses* and *Steptoe and Son* in quick succession… with significant rewards: *On the Buses* was the biggest UK box office hit of 71, even outgrossing the return of Connery as 007 in *Diamonds Are Forever*. Nor was the trend confined to raiding the sitcoms of a few years earlier. More cerebral adaptations included Monty Python's *And Now for Something Completely Different* and Edward Woodward in the downbeat spy drama *Callan*.

The 72 sequel to *Till Death Us Do Part* was directed by Bob Kellett and has the Garnett family relocated to a new housing estate in Hertfordshire, in circumstances that make for a curiously unhappy comparison with *Here We Go Round the Mulberry Bush*. It jettisons the political satire of the original TV series and opts instead for being a very mainstream UK film comedy revolving around the central character, Garnett/Mitchell, who even inadvertently takes LSD in one sequence. Both Una Stubbs and Anthony Booth declined to appear and the youth interest is maintained by their replacements, Adrienne Posta, who had co-starred in *Up the Junction*, and Paul Angelis, like Booth a scouser, and previously the voice of Ringo in *Yellow Submarine*. A large supporting cast featured many guest stars including Max Bygraves and George Best.

There are several discotheque and club sequences, one of which features Kenny Lynch performing with an as yet unidentified band. Lynch also did the main title theme. The remainder of the soundtrack was by Georgie Fame and Colin Green.

Released August 1972, 90 minutes, colour
DVD: Reissued in a double bill with *All The Way Up*, a 1970 film comedy starring Warren Mitchell in a non-Garnett role
SOUNDTRACK: No release

PINK FLOYD: LIVE AT POMPEII

Adrian Maben directs
Pink Floyd star

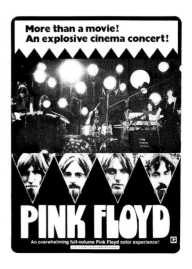

Before this 72 documentary, pop and rock stars usually appeared on film in a variety of guises: in inane reviews as one of several hopeful acts; in flimsy biographical stories about their own rise to fame; glimpsed in a dance hall/coffee bar/club; performing a title or theme song or acting in roles of various sizes and credibility. Sometimes combinations of these applied. Even the universal success of The Beatles and The Rolling Stones by the late 60s didn't really change these formulae: in *Let It Be*, The Beatles play their improvised street concert; in *Gimme Shelter*, The Rolling Stones are seen in extensive concert footage. *Pink Floyd: Live at Pompeii* is a very different matter: serious art, with the group as the sole and only focus of the film, performing, like high priests, in a Roman amphitheatre, and being treated, implicitly, as if they had the same status as Beethoven or Picasso.

A French-Belgian-West German production, shot at Pompeii in October 71 by Adrian Maben, the film is technically excellent and a significant benchmark in the career of the group, lifting them from a well known and successful rock band to megastars. The footage originally intended for release had them playing material from 'A Saucer Full of Secrets' and 'Meddle' but attempts to find a wide audience for this foundered when a premier at the Rainbow (in late 72) was cancelled on the basis it was a live music venue and not a cinema. (This was despite rock films commonly being shown as an ersatz gig at that time – Gentle Giant once toured as the support act to *Jimi Plays Berkeley*). To counter this, Maben added footage of the Floyd recording 'Dark Side of the Moon' and talking – at some length – in the canteen at the Abbey Road studios. The film thus exists in various versions, all of which have sold well.

There was no legitimate soundtrack release.

Released September 1972, 60 minutes, colour
DVD: Reissued by Universal, October 2003
SOUNDTRACK: No official release

Caroline Munro dancing to Stoneground

DRACULA AD 1972

Alan Gibson directs
Christopher Lee and Peter Cushing star

Given that it was produced by Michael Carreras – whose previous credits had included the script for the 66 Raquel Welch blockbuster *One Million Years BC* – *Dracula AD 1972* was never likely to be a literary masterpiece. An early 70s Hammer retread of the familiar vampire plot, this has the Count reappearing among Chelsea teenagers, practising black magic. Relocated to Swinging London, albeit at a time when the notion that such an entity existed was already in decline, the film was directed by Alan Gibson, who had also done *Goodbye Gemini*, which, like this, and the Italian/Spanish giallo *All the Colors of the Dark*, made six months earlier, concerns various diabolical goings-on somewhere near the Kings Road.

Hammer regulars Christopher Lee and Peter Cushing star, supported by Stephanie Beacham, whose earlier work included a role in *The Ballad of Tam Lin* and co-starring with Marlon Brando in Michael Winner's *The Nightcomers* (71). Actress and singer Marsha Hunt appears in a major supporting role.

The soundtrack was composed and arranged by Mike Vickers. Vickers, originally in the pop-jazz group Manfred Mann, had opted for a solo career early on: his work in film and TV included the theme music for the first adaptation of *Up the Junction*, and the soundtracks for the Norman Wisdom farce/political satire *Press for Time* and the Romy Schneider/Dennis Waterman drama *My Lover, My Son*. He could also make a fair claim, during this period, to the mantle of seminal UK pop-psych producer and arranger: among those benefitting from his touch in the studio being Cat Stevens, Duffy Power, Grapefruit, Kiki Dee, Paul Jones, The Scaffold, Tam White, Toby Twirl and The World of Oz. Here he deployed electronic music by White Noise, with an extended appearance from US group Stoneground, a ten piece 'hippy family' signed to Warner Brothers. Rumour has it that they replaced label mates The Faces, who were required to fulfil touring engagements during the couple of months it took to shoot the film.

Released September 1972, 96 minutes, colour
DVD: Reissued by Warner Brothers in October 2005
SOUNDTRACK: CD reissue in the US on BSX Records in 2009

DEATH LINE

Gary Sherman directs
Wil Malone does the music

Considered to be one of the great British horror films, *Death Line*, which starred Donald Pleasence and Norman Rossington, has a neat and simple plot that takes, as its premise, the existence of cannibalistic savages in the tube railway system beneath London, the survivors of a roof fall that trapped a group of railway passengers many years earlier. Co-star Sharon Gurney came from the cast of the pop musical *Catch My Soul* and had also appeared in several other horror films, notably *The Corpse* (71) and the Belgian *La Chambre Rouge* (72).

It was the first film of Gary Sherman (whom the BFI considered had made the directorial debut of the year) who came to it from a series of TV commercials, having previously filmed a number of US music shorts featuring The Seeds and Bo Diddley. Paul Maslansky produced, having previously done *Eyewitness*.

The soundtrack was composed by Jeremy Rose and Wil Malone and is now considered a worthy addition to Malone's highly regarded work, both as solo artist and with 60s psychedelic group Orange Bicycle. He would maintain his interest in film, with *That'll Be the Day* and *Jubilee* among his later screen credits. *Death Line* (renamed *Raw Meat* for its US release) did respectable business when shown in cinemas but remains a relatively little seen UK film of its era. The contemporary revival of interest in Wil Malone's music has resulted in the soundtrack becoming easily available on CD.

Released 1972, 87 minutes, colour
DVD: Released via Network in 2007
SOUNDTRACK LP/CD: Released on Spinney Records 2001

BORN TO BOOGIE

Ringo Starr directs
Marc Bolan stars

Starr and Bolan

After the April 70 announcement that The Beatles were breaking up, the UK media constantly sought, for some time thereafter, a new ensemble that could be proclaimed and anointed their heirs and successors. The emergence of T. Rex, in late 70, from the ashes of quirky psychedelic folk-pop duo Tyrannosaurus Rex, seemed the answer to their prayers: mass hysteria among teenage fans – particularly girls – resulting in six hit singles in eighteen months (including four UK number ones), a massive chart album, 'Electric Warrior', and, in early 72, the US breakthrough, with 'Get it On'.

Although a clear indication that the 60s were receding into the past and that a new chapter had opened in UK pop, and even though the musical style of Marc Bolan and his group was markedly different to the preceding genres of progressive rock, mainstream chart hits or even psychedelia (although ingredients of all three were clearly still present), the approach of the music industry to promoting its new stars remained the same: try and fit them into a feature film.

Thus emerged Born to Boogie, produced by Frank Simon, previously one of the cinematographers on Glastonbury Fayre, funded and distributed by Apple Corps and directed by Ringo Starr. Built around the March 72 Wembley concert headlined by T. Rex and Elton John and MC'd by outré DJ Emperor Rosko, and including an acoustic set filmed at John Lennon's Surrey mansion, the plot is decked out with various surrealist trimmings, so that the finished product resembles Magical Mystery Tour. On the acting side, Geoffrey Bayldon – best known for his work in the TV series Catweazle (about a mediaeval wizard transported to the late 60s) – appears.

Ringo also performs on the soundtrack – in an ad hoc supergroup with Bolan and Elton John. Ultimately, though, T. Rex were not 'the new Beatles'. Despite their LP 'The Slider' reaching number seventeen in the US in the autumn of 72, their star waned quite quickly and, by 74, 'Bolanmania' had dispersed. There were no sequel films.

**Released December 1972,
67 minutes, colour
DVD:** Reissued on Sanctuary in May 2006
SOUNDTRACK: LP released on Marc on Wax in 1991. CD reissue on Sanctuary Records in May 2005

PSYCHOMANIA

Don Sharp directs
Nicky Henson stars

A *tour de force*: part deadpan comedy and part counter-culture symbolism (with a setting that includes ritual magic and prehistoric monuments etc), *Psychomania* (aka *The Death Wheelers* in the USA) is efficiently directed by Don Sharp, whose previous credits included the UK rock and roll films *The Golden Disc* (57 – Terry Dene) and *It's All Happening* (62 – Tommy Steele), and is virtually the only example of a biker movie, a genre common in the US from *The Wild One* onwards, to emerge from a British film studio.

The plot concerns the leader of a Hells Angel gang, The Living Dead, who commits suicide with the foreknowledge that he can return from the grave. It stars Nicky Henson, who started his career as an EMI/Parlophone recording artist in the early 60s before moving into films with roles in *Here We Go Round the Mulberry Bush*, *The Jokers*, *30 is a Dangerous Age, Cynthia* and *There's a Girl in My Soup*, with George Sanders – whose last film this was – in support alongside Mary Larkin, Ann Michelle and Roy Holder, the latter also seen in *Loot*.

The soundtrack was put together by John Cameron, with help from modern jazz stalwarts Tony Carr and Harold McNair. Cameron worked extensively as an arranger with CCS, Jimmy Campbell, Lesley Duncan and The World of Oz and his music here includes a contribution from folk singer Harvey Andrews. An extract, 'Witch Hunt', credited to Frog, appeared on Jam Records in March 73.

Released March 1973, 95 minutes, colour
DVD: Reissued by Severin October 2010
SOUNDTRACK: Formal release on CD and LP in 2003 on Trunk Records

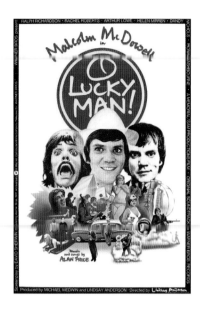

O LUCKY MAN!

Lindsay Anderson directs
Malcolm McDowell stars
Alan Price does the music

Before 'Love Me Do' wafted down from Merseyside and kicked off a new cultural era, UK intellectuals were much given to withering and critical looks at their own country. Books such as Michael Shanks' *The Stagnant Society* and the Arthur Koestler-edited *Suicide of a Nation* took the premise that something was very wrong with the state of the nation... and needed to be changed. This what's-wrong-with-Britain-theme was picked up by Lindsay Anderson and his screenplay writer, David Sherwin, in their Travis trilogy, which fired off broadsides at all parts of the political, social and economic establishment.

A long, enjoyable and picaresque production, *O Lucky Man!* was the second of these, continuing the adventures of the character played by Malcolm McDowell in 68's *If...* Described by one critic as 'a sort of mod Pilgrim's Progress', the film follows the career of Travis as a coffee salesman and international financier. Produced by Memorial, which had an outstanding run in UK cinema at this time with *Privilege*, *Charlie Bubbles*, *Spring and Port Wine* and *Gumshoe*, the film – despite its guying of others – fails to spell out an alternative to contemporary woes other than more love and liberalism and concludes with an extended scene where the cast come out of character and let their hair down, dancing to Alan Price and his band.

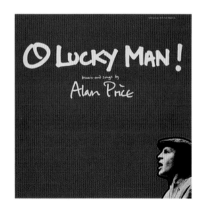

Price and his backing musicians Colin Green (guitar), Dave Markee (bass) and Clive Thacker (drums) appear and perform throughout the story, highlighting various moments in the plot. Their contribution was released as an LP on Warner Brothers, reaching number one hundred and seventeen in the US LP charts in late 73. With hindsight, *O Lucky Man!* may have been the last flowering of 60s optimism. Memorial withdrew from film production after the miserable near future drama *Memoirs of a Survivor* (81) and, by the time the third and final part of the Travis saga appeared, *Britannia Hospital* (82), the series was markedly less amusing and the UK was a very different country indeed.

Released March 1973, 183 minutes, colour
DVD: Reissued by Warner Home Video, May 2008
SOUNDTRACK: LP released by Warner Brothers 1973. CD reissue 1996

THAT'LL BE THE DAY

David Puttnam produces
Ringo Starr and David Essex star

Produced by EMI and Goodtimes Enterprises (David Puttnam's company, whose prior credits included *Performance*, *Melody* and *Glastonbury Fayre*), the main point of *That'll Be the Day* appears to have been the exploitation of the emerging fad for rock and roll nostalgia demonstrated by the success, in the US, of groups such as Sha Na Na, from 69, and the surprise charting of Elvis Presley classic *'Heartbreak Hotel'* in the UK when it was reissued in July 71.

A modest production that paired Ringo Starr with David Essex, the latter enjoying some success at the time as the star of the religious rock opera *Godspell*, the plot is about a young man (Essex) growing up in the fifties and quitting his limited working class life to be a pop star/rock and roll singer after enjoying a summer season working at a Butlins holiday camp. The film marked a major departure from the usual plot parameters of UK music films by being completely backward looking and unconcerned with anything contemporary. Astonishingly popular, the problem was – visually and artistically – it looked nothing like 58. The cast are too old, the cars and background detail are usually slightly wrong (in the real 50s much of the UK still looked like the 30s) and the soundtrack continually features music released after the period of the film. On close inspection even the clothes look suspect: too new, too tidy and too well cut. (The cast were actually dressed by Malcolm McLaren and Vivienne Westwood from the outfits devised and stocked by them in their Kings Road boutique, *Let It Rock*). For audiences agog with a desire for escapist entertainment in the increasingly beleaguered and dreary UK of the early 70s, none of this mattered, nor seemingly did the elementary observation that David Essex wasn't a particularly interesting figure to build the film around. In a brief cameo, Billy Fury, with barely a line of dialogue, knocks spots off him. Filmed in the late summer of 72, it was followed by a hopeful *Melody Maker* announcement, a few months later, that Graham Bond would be composing the soundtrack. In the event Bond, then in the last stages of heroin addiction and with a heavy interest in the occult, was not called upon to do this; though he does appear in the film – as the saxophone player in Billy Fury's group – looking, as does John Hawken (on keyboards, and ex-Renaissance), like a refugee from a contemporary prog-rock band.

The original music in the film was scored and produced by Wil Malone and played by Bond, Hawken, Fury, Jack Bruce, Steve Winwood and Jim Capaldi (Traffic), Keith Moon and Pete Townshend (The Who), Ron Wood, Keith Richards and Viv Stanshall. Accomplished, brilliant even, in parts (such as Fury's rendition of Townshend's *'Long Live Rock'*), it still sounded, of course, nothing like the late 50s. The soundtrack LP, which appeared on the budget label Ronco, also included, alongside the original material and many greatest hits of 'the rock and roll era', a cover version of *'It'll Be Me'* by UK paisley pop act Wishful Thinking, who also appear in the film. It hit number one in the UK album chart in June 73, holding this position for seven weeks until replaced by the latest Peters and Lee release.

Released April 1973, 91 minutes, colour
DVD: Reissued by Warner Home Video, August 2003
SOUNDTRACK: Double LP released on Ronco in 1973

THE FINAL PROGRAMME

Robert Fuest directs
Jon Finch stars

Much of 60s pop culture took its inspiration from the strip cartoon. At a grand level this was seen with the iconic images of Roy Lichtenstein (notably *Wham!* [exhibited to acclaim in 63]) whilst cinematically the form gave birth to *Modesty Blaise* (film 66, cartoon 63), *Jeu de Massacre* (film 67, images by Guy Peellaert), *Danger Diabolik!* and *Barbarella* (both filmed 68 from comics that appeared in 62). The trend also produced *The Final Programme* an entry from the UK counter-culture via Michael Moorcock, one of the major literary figures of the period. Based on his 68 novel and intended as an outrageous parody of 007, it was serialised as a comic strip in *International Times*, circa 71. The plot is centred on the escapades of Jerry Cornelius, a Swinging London figure in a crushed velvet suit and ruffled shirt (the credits state that costumes were provided by Ossie Clark and Tommy Nutter), who lives somewhere near Ladbroke Grove, drives a massive US car equipped with its own stereo system blasting out The Who, Zoot Money's Big Roll Band and The Beatles, lives on a diet of pills and alcohol, seems to be some type of secret agent and spends most of his time in discotheques and boutiques. Cornelius, and variations of his character, were still appearing in new works by Moorcock thirty years later.

As directed by Robert Fuest, whose previous credits included the advertising satire *Just Like a Woman*, the film that emerges could easily have been a remarkable *tour de force*, but plays instead as a medium speed, slightly wacky upmarket version of *Dr Who*, decked out with sex scenes. It was disowned by Moorcock and offers a strange melange of

THE END–

OR THE BEGINNING?

The FiNAL PROGRAMME

THE FINAL PROGRAMME. Starring Jon Finch as being Cornelius Jenny Runacre
Sterling Hayden · Harry Andrews · Hugh Griffith · Graham Crowden · Julie Ege and Patrick Magee
Produced by JOHN GOLDSTONE and SANDY LIEBERSON · Designed, written and directed by ROBERT FUEST · Technicolor® · Distributed by Anglo EMI Film Distributors Limited

themes: part bleak sci-fi (shot in derelict areas near the Westway), part druggy comedy whilst drawing heavily on one of the key hippy texts of the era, Pauwels and Bergier's *The Dawn of Magic* (aka *The Morning of the Magicians* in the USA), with a sub-plot about secret Nazi U-boat bases at the North Pole guarding the entrance to the Hollow Earth. Rather curiously, when distributed in the US by Anglo-EMI (who had previously made the Frankie Howerd farce *Up the Chastity Belt*), the film was renamed *The Last Days of Man on Earth*, with publicity material that suggested it was something to do with the *Planet of the Apes* franchise. The main role is played by Jon Finch – Mick Jagger, smarting from the critical thumbs down to *Ned Kelly*, turned down the part, stating that it was 'too weird' – supported by Jenny Runacre and a gallery of dependable UK character actors. The plot? It's something about a mad scientist creating a self-reproducing hermaphrodite as the end of the world approaches.

For the soundtrack Moorcock wanted, and got, Hawkwind, only for their involvement to be restricted to a three minute instrumental track decking out a scene shot in what appears to be a psychedelic amusement arcade. They can – just – be glimpsed in the background. The remainder of the music, by Bernard Krause, is mainly electronic with some additional contributions by jazz saxophonist Gerry Mulligan.

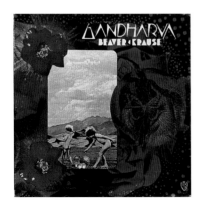

Released October 1973, 94 minutes, colour
DVD: Reissued by Anchor Bay, June 2001
SOUNDTRACK: No official release

Christopher Lee brings things to a conclusion

THE WICKER MAN

Robin Hardy directs
Edward Woodward, Christopher Lee and Britt Ekland star

Regarded now as the definitive example of a UK horror film, *The Wicker Man*, like *The Tragedy of Macbeth*, *The Ballad of Tam Lin* and the Italian/French/German giallo thriller *Seven Dead in the Cat's Eye* (72 – with Jane Birkin), was filmed on location in Scotland. Produced by Peter Snell, whose earlier credits included the spy thriller *Subterfuge* (68) and *Goodbye Gemini* and directed by Robin Hardy – whose subsequent cinema career was surprisingly slight – it was scripted by Anthony Shaffer, then enjoying a major success with the play and film adaptation of *Sleuth*.

The plot takes a serious look at the difference between Christian and pre-Christian faiths and centres on a policeman investigating the disappearance of a child on a remote Scottish island, only to find he has been deliberately trapped and will be offered as a sacrifice by the local inhabitants who have retained their pagan beliefs. A strong cast is headed by Edward Woodward, Christopher Lee, Ingrid Pitt and Britt Ekland. Mime artist Lindsay Kemp, who performed with David Bowie circa 69, appears in a minor role. The film was mildly successful when released (David McGillivray stating it to be '… an encouraging achievement for those who had begun to despair of the British cinema…'), only to be neglected subsequently before receiving great acclaim in the 90s.

Woodward was something of a box office draw at this point, with starring roles in *The File of the Golden Goose* (69) and *Sitting Target* (72) as well as the immensely popular TV series *Callan*. He also had a successful singing career, recording for DJM as a kind of very English MOR version of Scott Walker. The soundtrack, by US playwright, actor and musician Paul Giovanni, draws on various influences and has become a classic of psych-folk.

Released December 1973, 88 minutes, colour
DVD: Reissued by Optimum Home Entertainment, October 2006
SOUNDTRACK: CD release on Trunk Records, 1998

The Connoisseur's Guide to 60s Pop Film Music...

A PUTATIVE TOP 20

John Barry 'The Knack'
main theme from *THE KNACK*

Julie Driscoll and the Don Ellis Orchestra
'Moon Zero Two'
from *MOON ZERO TWO*

Mark Murphy 'Ain't That Just Like a Woman'
from *JUST LIKE A WOMAN*

George Harrison and The Remo Four
'Wonderwall to be here'
from *WONDERWALL*

Phillip Goodhand-Tait 'Cold Night'
from *UNIVERSAL SOLDIER*

Peter and Gordon 'The Jokers'
from *THE JOKERS*

Don Partridge 'Homeless Bones'
from *OTLEY*

Georgie Fame 'Entertaining Mr Sloane'
from *ENTERTAINING MR SLOANE*

Gianni Davoli 'Love Girl'
from *COL CUORE IN GOLA*

The Kinks 'The March of the Virgin Soldiers'
from *THE VIRGIN SOLDIERS*

The Peddlers 'Tell The World We're Not In'
from *GOODBYE GEMINI*

Yvonne 'I'm So Young'
from *SMASHING TIME*
(OK – She's not a real pop singer, but it's brilliant)

Dusty Springfield 'The Corrupt Ones'
from *THE CORRUPT ONES*

The Freedom 'Attraction'
from *NEROSUBIANCO*

Pink Floyd 'Cirrus Minor'
from *MORE*

The Beatles 'I am the Walrus'
from *MAGICAL MYSTERY TOUR*

Manfred Mann 'Up the Junction'
from *UP THE JUNCTION*

JP Rags 'If It's Tuesday, This Must Be Belgium'
from *IF IT'S TUESDAY, THIS MUST BE BELGIUM*

Andy Ellison 'It's Been a Long Time'
from *HERE WE GO ROUND THE MULBERRY BUSH*

The Electric Banana 'Eagle's Son'
from *WHAT'S GOOD FOR THE GOOSE*

ZARDOZ

John Boorman directs
Sean Connery and Charlotte Rampling star

Sean Connery dressed to kill in the 23rd century

Following his critical success with *Leo the Last*, John Boorman spent 70 and 71 in the US, working on a counter-culture adaptation of *The Lord of The Rings*. Alas United Artists, who had purchased the film rights from JRR Tolkien in 69, baulked at funding such a sprawling project, particularly one in which the hobbits take magic mushrooms. Having had a commercial tour de force with *Deliverance*, Boorman relocated to the UK, or, more precisely the British Isles – he filmed most of it in Ireland – where he made *Zardoz*. It represented a somewhat endangered species within the UK film industry when it appeared in 74: an ambitious and completely original script, filmed with a star cast and adequate funding.

Starring Sean Connery and Charlotte Rampling, and with John Alderton, from the TV series *Please Sir!* in support, the film resembles *A Clockwork Orange* and *The Final Programme* with its dystopian view of the future. Set in the twenty-third century, after an unspecified environmental catastrophe has wiped out most of the human race, the story focuses on a small elite group of survivors who reside within a hermetically sealed bubble, with the wastelands beyond this patrolled by vigilantes whose task is to destroy anyone they encounter. Connery – clad in thigh-high leather boots and orange jock strap, sporting a Zapata moustache and ponytail and carrying a British army service revolver – leads the latter and breaks into the survivors' community with predictably severe results for those concerned.

An entertaining and well made film, *Zardoz* came with a soundtrack from David Munrow, who had provided the musical background for the memorable 68 BBC radio adaptation of *The Hobbit*, and whose previous work included the soundtrack to *The Devils*, collaborations with Shirley and Dolly Collins, The Young Tradition and The Round Table and leading The Early Music Consort of London. Mixing folk and classical, the score also includes a contribution from jazz-funk act Zzebra.

Released February 1974, 105 minutes, colour
DVD: Reissued by Twentieth Century Fox Home Entertainment June 2003
SOUNDTRACK: Limited to a single released by Zzebra on Polydor in March 1974

Jodorowsky

If contenders were sought for the hippiest, trippiest film project of the era – a field which would boast several worthy candidates – the prize would surely be awarded to Alejandro Jodorowsky's *Dune*, which flared briefly into life for a couple of years in the mid 70s. Based on one of the seminal counter-culture texts of the time, a four hundred and fifty page science fiction doorstopper set twenty one thousand years in the future, the first stab at turning it into a film followed the euphoria that greeted Kubrick's success with *2001: A Space Odyssey* and came from Arthur P Jacobs, producer of the huge hit *Planet of the Apes*. He found easier goals to pursue, and the chalice passed instead to Jodorowsky who enjoyed, at this point, a reputation as a cutting edge *auteur*, particularly with George Harrison and John Lennon. His 70 western, *El Topo*, was distributed by Apple in the US, its score was rerecorded for release, on Apple, by John Barham, a long term collaborator of theirs (some would say he had superseded George Martin in this role) whilst his next project, *The Holy Mountain*, during which he took LSD and underwent sensory deprivation, was produced and part funded by Allen Klein.

After an abortive attempt – also with Klein and Apple – at bringing *The Story of O* to the screen, two years of preparatory work commenced on *Dune*, during which it ballooned into something that would out-Kubrick Kubrick with a cast that, at various times, included Mick Jagger, Charlotte Rampling (whom Jodorowsky had admired in *Zardoz*), Alain Delon, David Carradine (then a big hit in the TV series *Kung Fu*), Orson Welles and Salvador Dali. Elaborate sets were created by HR Giger (who designed the sleeve for the 73 Emerson, Lake and Palmer LP *'Brain Salad Surgery'*), each scene in the plot was drawn and storyboarded by Chris Foss, otherwise known

Alejandro Jodorowsky as El Topo.

ALEXANDRO
JODOROWSKY

DUNE

FRANK HERBERT

MICHEL SEYDOUX

as the illustrator of *The Joy of Sex*, whilst the
script, by Dan O'Bannon, who had just written
the critically acclaimed *Dark Star*, was so long
that, when released, *Dune* would have had
a running time of fourteen hours, making its
near contemporary *Fata Morgana* look like
a soap powder commercial by comparison.
Practicalities were clearly not an issue, as it was
intended to spend a year filming on location in
the Sahara Desert. Most intriguing of all were the
arrangements for the soundtrack – Jodorowsky
wanted a different band for each planet. Virgin
Records offered Gong, Mike Oldfield, Henry Cow
and Tangerine Dream. German avant-gardist
Karlheinz Stockhausen and French prog-rockers
Magma were also postulated, until the mantle
settled on Pink Floyd – for what would have been
their tenth feature film credit.

But Jodorowsky never made *Dune*, never even
started it in fact, as production was abandoned
after $2m had been spent without a single
frame being shot. Such extravagance is seen,
today, retrospectively, as somehow emblematic
of an era when budgets were out of control and
there was inadequate planning and financial
discipline. But is this true? Was *Dune* an
overblown ludicrous cod epic? The mid 70s
preproduction costs of $2m (£900k at the time)
equate to roughly £9m today. In a world where
a film like *Avatar* can cost $237m (£166m),
with at least ten per cent being spent on
preproduction, the failure of *Dune* looks more
like a doomed attempt to create a massively
complex production at a time when the
technology for this simply hadn't been invented;
typical, instead, of an era when ambition and
optimism didn't recognise limitations. Even
the running time of fourteen hours looks
unexceptional today in a world of mini-series
and franchise films. (Coincidentally, both
O'Bannon and Giger were involved in *Alien* and
its many sequels from 78-79 onwards). Perhaps,
now that the concept of anything being
'unfilmable' no longer exists, the final judgement
might be that Jodorowsky was forty years ahead
of his time.

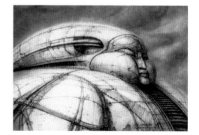

HR Giger's artwork for Dune

STARDUST

David Essex stars
Dave Edmunds does the music

With a film poster asking Remember the 60s? which, given it appeared only five years after the end of the decade, could be said to demonstrate how that era was already regarded by many in the early 70s as a now lost, carefree period of opportunity and prosperity, *Stardust* was the sequel to *That'll Be the Day*. It starred David Essex, reprising his earlier role, supported by Adam Faith, Marty Wilde and Larry Hagman – the latter possibly cast in the expectation that his appearance might open up the US market. Ringo Starr declined to appear, reasoning that, as an ex-Beatle, his appearance as anyone else in a film about the 60s pop scene might baffle watchers.

The view that the film takes of the UK music industry is suitably cynical, and similar in tone to that taken by contemporary TV series like *The Sweeney* about their subject matter. Like *That'll Be the Day*, though, the plot is entirely backwards looking and nostalgic and contains its fair share of incongruities: the audience is asked to believe that the character played by Essex has a fan club with three million members (making him possibly the most successful pop star in the world) whilst the music he plays and sings – though accurate/adequate – is really no more than a pastiche of the styles of the time and would have made him an interesting minor success, at best, during the period itself.

The score was delegated to Dave Edmunds (formerly of Love Sculpture and shortly to be a seminal figure in the rise of the UK New Wave), assisted by Nick Lowe (uncredited), Keith Moon, Paul Nicholas, Jeff Wayne and Gary Osborne, the last a former member of the UK version of The Chocolate Watch Band. The original material was duly released, amidst a huge array of 'greatest hits' from the 60s portrayed, on a quadruple LP, by budget label Ronco… but failed, unlike its predecessor, to sell, though David Essex took the sombre title song 'Stardust' to number seven in the UK singles chart at the end of 74. Some of Edmunds' work was released on his own label, Rockfield, in 74-75.

Released March 1974, 111 minutes, colour
DVD: Reissued by Warner Home Video, August 2003
SOUNDTRACK: LP release on Ronco 1974, no subsequent reissue

SON OF DRACULA (COUNT DOWNE)

Freddie Francis directs
Nilsson stars and does the music

Originally advertised in the trade press in 70 as *Count Downe*, a conventional horror film starring Dennis Price, by the time shooting commenced in August 72 this had metamorphosed into *Son of Dracula* – a shambling rock musical, funded and produced by Apple Corps.

Directed by Freddie Francis, whose other work included the horror films *Trog* and *Mumsy, Nanny, Sonny and Girly*, as well as being the cinematographer on *Saturday Night and Sunday Morning* and much else, it starred Harry Nilsson and Ringo Starr, with Starr also co-producing and editing the film. The supporting cast was headed by Price who – like George Sanders in *Psychomania* – died before the film was released. A heavily indulgent rock and roll version of the Dracula story, it features a huge array of musicians: Peter Frampton, John Bonham, Leon Russell and Keith Moon are all prominent, as is Shakira Caine (wife of Michael) in a supporting role.

Nilsson did most of the soundtrack, which was cobbled together with material from two of his earlier LPs together with a brilliant new song 'Daybreak' which, when released as a single, reached number thirty nine in the US charts, in March 74. The arrangements and orchestrations came from Paul Buckmaster whose other work included collaborations with Arrival, Elton John, Michael Chapman and David Bowie.

Released April 1974, 90 minutes, colour
DVD: Video release reputed to have taken place in the US. No official DVD reissue
SOUNDTRACK: LP release – on Rapple Records – 1974. No subsequent reissue

LITTLE MALCOLM AND HIS STRUGGLE AGAINST THE EUNUCHS

John Hurt and David Warner star in the final Apple production

One of the most enduring literary tropes of the 50s and 60s was the 'angry young man', brought to mass audiences in *Look Back in Anger* (play 56 – film 59 with Richard Burton and music by Chris Barber) and *Saturday Night and Sunday Morning* (book 58 – film 60 with Albert Finney and music by Johnny Dankworth). Usually a student, firmly anti-establishment and existing on the margins – an attic bedsit, a diet of cigarettes and ad hoc meals, fond of pubs and jazz – the type was rebooted (and relocated to Swinging London) in *Morgan – A Suitable Case for Treatment* (TV 62 – film 66 with David Warner and music by Dankworth) and by Dick Clement and Ian La Frenais in the 67 BBC TV adaptation of *The Further Adventures of Lucky Jim* (theme song by Alan Price). Its last blast came with this, a hugely popular play, written by David Halliwell and originally staged by Mike Leigh in 65, with John Hurt and Rodney Bewes. George Harrison saw it early in its run and optioned it as a potential film… but Apple, using the profits from *Yellow Submarine*, took until 74 to get it onto the cinema screens. It proved to be the final film project from The Beatles company, and ironically (and with the benefit of hindsight), brought to an end the era of semi-obligatory pop and rock participation in UK cinema that the Fab Four themselves had launched a decade earlier.

Stuart Cooper, who had previously done a documentary on the Australian painter Sidney Nolan, directed from a script by Derek Woodward – coincidentally, just seen as a werewolf in *Son of Dracula*. A satire on fascism, and how it can arise from mundane and banal circumstances, it stars John Hurt, David Warner and John McEnery, decked out in flares, greatcoats and festooned with facial hair, as fiercely

John Hurt as Little Malcolm

political art students in a northern college plotting revenge on the authorities after one of them (Hurt) is expelled. Filmed on location in Oldham, during the miserable winter of 73 (in a complex of buildings in a disused gas works), it failed to ignite at the UK box office despite winning an award at the Berlin Film Festival. After a cursory showing at one London cinema, it was withdrawn from release and, thereafter, only screened by George Harrison as an after dinner event at his Surrey mansion – leading some wags to describe it as the most expensive home movie ever made.

Harrison both co-produced (with Gavrik Losey) and did the soundtrack which contains incidental music by him (assisted by Pete Ham of Badfinger and Billy Preston) and a theme song co-written by Mal Evans, a longstanding Beatles assistant and collaborator. This is performed by Splinter, a band whose singer Bill Elliott had previously released 'Oh God Save Us' (as Bill Elliot and The Elastic Oz Band), a benefit single on Apple for Oz magazine during their obscenity trial in 71.

Released July 1974, 109 minutes, colour
DVD: Reissued by BFI Video, October 2011
SOUNDTRACK: No formal release

APPENDIX 1

Other Feature Films

DOCTOR IN CLOVER

Penultimate in the popular UK comedy series. Theme song was performed by Kiki Dee. (March 66)

SMOKE OVER LONDON (FUMO DI LONDRA)

Vehicle for Italian comic actor Alberto Sordi who wrote and directed. Dana Gillespie appears in a small role. Soundtrack has two songs by Julie Rogers. (66)

AFTER THE FOX

US/Italian comedy caper. Folk singer Shawn Phillips appears in a minor role. Theme song by Peter Sellers and The Hollies, released as a single. (September 66)

MADE IN U.S.A.

Jean-Luc Godard feature, starring Anna Karina. Marianne Faithfull appears singing 'As Tears Go By'. (December 66)

THE CORRUPT ONES (DIE HÖLLE VON MACAO)

Spy drama shot in Germany and Hong Kong with Elke Sommer and Robert Stack. Title song by Dusty Springfield. (January 67)

STRANGER IN THE HOUSE

US Crime drama shot in the UK. Eric Burdon and The

Animals perform 'Ain't that so' on soundtrack. (May 67)

TWO WEEKS IN SEPTEMBER

Brigitte Bardot drama filmed in London. Mike Sarne and Murray Head in the supporting cast, both playing photographers à la David Hemmings in *Blow-Up*. (June 67)

KILL ME QUICK, I'M COLD
(FAI IN FRETTA AD UCCIDERMI... HO FREDDO!)

Italian crime caper starring Monica Vitti. Title song by The Hollies. (September 67)

HOUSE OF 1000 DOLLS

German/Spanish crime/horror film starring Vincent Price with Caroline Coon in a minor role. Title theme by the Cliff Bennett Band. (November 67)

THE BIGGEST BUNDLE OF THEM ALL

US/Italian crime drama with a title song performed by Eric Burdon and The Animals. (January 68)

THE ANNIVERSARY

Hammer black comedy starring Bette Davis. The New Vaudeville Band perform the main theme song. (February 68)

THE LOST CONTINENT

Hammer horror based on a Dennis Wheatley book and set in the Sargasso Sea. Dana Gillespie appears in a minor role. The Peddlers perform on the soundtrack. (June 68)

THE MINI WEEKEND

Early Tigon exploitation piece with similar plot to *Alfie*. Him and the Others appear in a discotheque scene. (June 68)

THE SWEET RIDE

Surfing drama shot in Malibu with Jacqueline Bisset. Dusty Springfield sings the title song which was written by Lee Hazlewood. (June 68)

INADMISSIBLE EVIDENCE

UK film version of a John Osborne play. Soundtrack by Dudley Moore. (68)

SPIRITS OF THE DEAD

Portmanteau part-directed by Fellini whose sequence stars Terence Stamp and features Liverpool group The Motowns, who like The Renegades, Mal and the Primitives and The Casuals had relocated to Italy. (68)

HOT MILLIONS

US Comedy drama starring Peter Ustinov that was filmed in London – including a sequence in the Apple Boutique in Baker Street, London W1. Lulu sang the main theme song. (September 68)

IF...

Fiercely political counter-culture satire of the English class system, directed by Lindsay Anderson. It's not really a 'pop' film but it has some freewheeling psychedelic moments and propelled

Malcolm McDowell to a brief period as a UK box office star and got him the lead in *A Clockwork Orange*. One item from the soundtrack, an obscure Belgian recording of *'Missa Luba'* by Les Troubadours du Roi Baudouin, was released as a single in the UK and reached number twenty eight in the charts. (December 68)

WHERE'S JACK?

A late entry in the genre that mined the seam exploited by *Tom Jones*, *The Amorous Adventures of Moll Flanders* and *Lock Up Your Daughters*. Set in the eighteenth century and stars Tommy Steele. Title song by Mary Hopkin. (April 69)

MACHINE GUN MCCAIN
(GLI INTOCCABILI)

Italian crime drama with title theme by Jackie Lynton. (April 69)

THE ITALIAN JOB

Arguably one of the most iconic UK productions of the 60s – but not really a Swinging London film and with no discernible pop music input. DJ Simon Dee appears in a small supporting role. (June 69)

HAMLET

Heavyweight UK production with Marianne Faithfull in a supporting role. (September 69)

ALL NEAT IN BLACK STOCKINGS

UK comedy about a window cleaner and his adventures in Swinging London. Theme song by Jon Mark. (September 69)

SKOTTET

Swedish drama about teenagers messing about with drugs and guns. Film contains a musical contribution from Mandrake Paddle Steamer. (September 69)

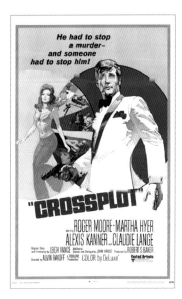

CROSSPLOT

London-set spy drama, with a pre-Bond Roger Moore. Lois Lane appears in a minor role. (November 69)

KES

Neither a pop film nor in any way connected to Swinging London but a significant UK film

event of the time nonetheless. Made by Ken Loach after his successes with *Cathy Come Home* (TV) and *Poor Cow*, it shows the bleak side of the industrial north in the late 60s, focusing on a boy's relationship with his pet falcon. Soundtrack was done by John Cameron and an ensemble led by Harold McNair and Tony Carr – all three being closely involved with Donovan during this period. (November 69)

RED SUN

A very significant West German drama involving murder, revolutionary politics and the counter-culture that stars Uschi Obermaier, member of Amon Düül, a radical Munich commune, and one time girlfriend of Jimi Hendrix. The soundtrack includes material by The Nice as well as The Small Faces performing *'Ogdens' Nut Gone Flake'*. (70)

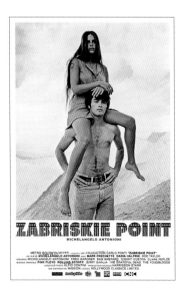

ZABRISKIE POINT

Quintessential US hippy road movie, directed by Michelangelo Antonioni as his follow-up to *Blow-Up*. The soundtrack contains two contributions from Pink Floyd (*'Crumbling Land'* and *'Heart Beat, Pig Meat'*) as well as The Rolling Stones *'You Got The Silver'*. (February 70)

MY LOVER MY SON

US/UK drama centred on an inappropriate family relationship. Soundtrack by Mike Vickers. (May 70)

THE STRAWBERRY STATEMENT

Drama about unrest on a US campus. Soundtrack includes Thunderclap Newman performing *'Something in the Air'*. (June 70)

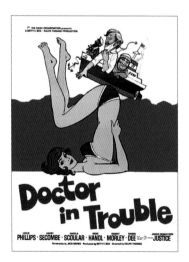

DOCTOR IN TROUBLE

Final entry in the popular UK comedy series. Simon Dee appears in a supporting role. (June 70)

TIRETANA

US/Spanish action film, supposedly set in Kashmir. Soundtrack by Mike Vickers. (70)

ALL THE WAY UP

Comedy about a ruthless social climber, played by Warren Mitchell. Title song by The Scaffold. (June 70)

EVERY HOME SHOULD HAVE ONE

Marty Feldman comedy, with Dave Dee in a small supporting role. (June 70)

SALOME

Spanish independent film version of Oscar Wilde play. Soundtrack claims to include an arrangement (by Jorge Pi of Desde Santurce A Bilbao Blues Band) of Pink Floyd arranged version of Richard Strauss composition *'Salome'*. (70)

NED KELLY

Drama about outlaw, filmed in Australia and starring Mick Jagger – who also declaims *'Wild Colonial Boy'* on the soundtrack LP. (July 70)

TOOMORROW

Students form a band and get involved with an alien landing on Earth. Pop musical starring Olivia Newton-John. (August 70)

THE RAGING MOON

Romance about love affair between two disabled people. Soundtrack includes a contribution from Blue Mink. (January 71)

PLEASE SIR!

Film version of popular TV series that was itself a spin-off from *To Sir, With Love*. Soundtrack by Mike Vickers includes a song by Cilla Black. (71)

ASSAULT

Thriller with David Essex in a small role. (February 71)

GET CARTER

Classic UK crime drama, filmed on Tyneside with a strikingly sparse musical soundtrack by Roy Budd. (February 71)

TAKING OFF

First US feature from exiled Czech director Milos Forman. Soundtrack includes The Incredible String Band. (March 71)

UP THE CHASTITY BELT

Frankie Howerd follow-up to *Up Pompeii* feature film version

of TV series. Long John Baldry appears in a small acting role. Soundtrack includes song written by Ken Howard and Alan Blaikley and performed by Eartha Kitt and a contribution from early 60s satirist David Kernan. (71)

ZEPPELIN

World War One adventure. Soundtrack by Roy Budd. (April 71)

DUSTY AND SWEETS MCGEE

Drama about heroin addiction. Soundtrack includes a contribution from Van Morrison. (71)

DAVID AND THE ICE AGE

West German film about a hippie dropping out. Rod Stewart can be heard on the soundtrack, which also includes material by Popol Vuh. (June 71)

SUNDAY BLOODY SUNDAY

John Schlesinger drama about a three-way relationship. Features Murray Head in a major starring role and has a soundtrack by Ron Geesin. (July 71)

THE LAST REBEL

Spaghetti western with a soundtrack by Ashton, Gardner and Dyke and Jon Lord. (September 71)

COME TOGETHER

Road movie filmed in Italy and Spain and produced by Ringo Starr and Allen Klein. Filmed back to back with *Blindman*. (September 71)

AND NOW FOR SOMETHING COMPLETELY DIFFERENT

Collection of sketches from the 69 and 70 Monty Python's Flying Circus series, put together for cinema showing by the BBC. Not strictly a pop film – but its reliance on animation sequences and surreal humour make it a kind of distant cousin to *Sgt. Pepper*. The soundtrack makes heavy usage of the De Wolfe Music Library, with pieces by Reg Tilsley, John Hawksworth, Simon Park and Stanley Black. (September 71)

BLINDMAN

Spaghetti western produced by Allen Klein and starring Ringo Starr. (November 1971)

THE MAGNIFICENT SEVEN DEADLY SINS

Comedy compendium film with an episode for each of the seven deadly sins. Soundtrack by Roy Budd, who also wrote the film theme song performed by Middle of the Road. (November 71)

200 MOTELS

Sprawling US/UK feature about Frank Zappa and his band touring the US. Ringo Starr and Keith Moon also appear. (November 71)

BAD MAN'S RIVER

Spanish/Italian/French spaghetti western with a soundtrack by Waldo de los Rios and UK prog rock band Jade Warrior. (December 71)

KIDNAPPED

Filmed on location in Scotland and starring Michael Caine, this version of the Robert Louis Stevenson adventure has a soundtrack by Roy Budd and a main theme song by Mary Hopkin. (December 71)

GUMSHOE

Albert Finney comedy drama about a bingo caller in a northern town who becomes a Humphrey Bogart-style private detective. The Roy Young Band appears on the soundtrack. (December 71)

ZEE AND CO

Elizabeth Taylor and Michael Caine drama about a failing marriage, from a novel by Edna O'Brien. Soundtrack by Rick Wakeman, also includes contributions by The Roy Young Band. (January 72)

FOR THE LOVE OF ADA

Comedy adapted from a 70 ITV series. Title theme by Gilbert O'Sullivan. (72)

BURKE AND HARE

UK horror film with title song by The Scaffold. (72)

BROTHER SUN, SISTER MOON

Franco Zeffirelli biographical study of St. Francis of Assisi. Soundtrack written and recorded by Donovan. (March 72)

JACK'S WIFE

Also known as *Season of the Witch*. George A Romero horror film about an unhappy suburban housewife. Title song performed by Donovan. (May 72)

ALL COPPERS ARE...

Working class drama set in south London. David Essex appears in a supporting role. (June 72)

UMANO NON UMANO

Italian documentary by artist Mario Schifano that includes appearances by Mick Jagger and Keith Richards and has material by The Rolling Stones on its soundtrack. (72)

OH! CALCUTTA

Film version of the Kenneth Tynan nude revue/musical. Includes material written by John Lennon. (June 72)

BENJAMIN

West German film with a soundtrack by Gary Wright of Spooky Tooth. (October 72)

HAPKIDO

Martial arts war film made in Hong Kong. Soundtrack includes Emerson, Lake and Palmer. (October 72)

THE ADVENTURES OF BARRY MCKENZIE

Comedy about an Australian visiting London. Julie Covington appears in a supporting role and also performs a song. (October 72)

HEAT

Andy Warhol parody of *Sunset Boulevard*. Soundtrack by John Cale. (October 72)

IMAGES

Hemdale-produced UK/US thriller, filmed in London and Ireland. Soundtrack includes music by Stomu Yamashta. (November 72)

THE PIED PIPER

UK version of the Grimm Brothers fairy tale, starring Donovan, who also does the soundtrack. (December 72)

TEMPTATION IN THE SUMMER WIND

German film comedy, with Sandie Shaw in a supporting role. (December 72)

THE MOTHER AND THE WHORE

French love triangle drama. Soundtrack includes Deep Purple performing *'Concerto for Group and Orchestra'*. (May 73)

THE DOLL SQUAD

B-movie about the CIA using four women secret agents to save the world from various threats. Theme song by Solomon King. (September 73)

APPENDIX 2

Documentaries
and Concert Films

Bob Dylan in Don't Look Back

DON'T LOOK BACK

Albert Grossman-produced and DA Pennebaker-directed documentary about Bob Dylan touring the UK in 65. As well as footage of Dylan and Joan Baez, Donovan, John Mayall, Alan Price, Marianne Faithfull and Brian Pendleton (The Pretty Things) are all seen. (May 67)

DOPE

Feature length documentary – filmed in London – about a young girl who succumbs to drugs. Also known as *Boots at Midnight*, Marianne Faithfull appears, playing herself, and the footage includes an early 67 two minute segment of Pink Floyd playing at the UFO Club. (68)

MONTEREY POP

Feature film length documentary about the first major rock festival, held at Monterey, California in June 67. Directed by DA Pennebaker and produced by Lou Adler and John Phillips, it set the template in tone and style for many similar ventures that followed. Whilst showcasing many (incomparable) US acts, it also includes footage of Eric Burdon and The Animals, The Who, The Jimi Hendrix Experience and (glimpsed in the audience) Brian Jones. (December 68)

Jimi Hendrix in Monterey Pop

FAREWELL CONCERT

Tony Palmer BBC TV documentary of the last gig played by Cream – at the Albert Hall in November 68, supported by Yes. (January 69)

POPCORN

Footage of Eric Burdon and The Animals, The Bee Gees, Joe Cocker, The Vanilla Fudge, Traffic, Jimi Hendrix, The Rolling Stones, Twiggy and Otis Redding, spliced together from various sources by Peter Clifton. (November 69)

WOODSTOCK

Michael Wadleigh directed concert documentary covering the 69 Woodstock Festival. Aside from many US acts, includes footage of The Who, Joe Cocker, Ten Years After and Jimi Hendrix. (March 70)

COLOSSEUM AND JUICY LUCY

Tony Palmer directed concert documentary, showcasing Colosseum and Juicy Lucy. (70)

5 + 1

French documentary, containing footage of two concerts: Johnny Hallyday (Paris, March 69) and The Rolling Stones (Hyde Park, July 69). (June 70)

LISTENING TO YOU – THE WHO AT THE ISLE OF WIGHT

Coverage of the 70 Isle of Wight Festival that, as well as focusing on The Who, includes footage of Taste and Jimi Hendrix. (August 70)

EXPERIENCE

Documentary short about The Jimi Hendrix Experience, originally made in 68 by Peter Neal – who later worked on *Be Glad for the Song Has No Ending* and *Glastonbury Fayre* – that appeared after Hendrix died, with a narration by Alexis Korner. (October 70)

LONDON ROCK

TV documentary about the London counter-culture that contains performances from Rod Stewart and The Faces, Fairport Convention and Linda Lewis, an interview with Marc Bolan and footage of the 70 Glastonbury Festival. (70)

REGGAE

The first major documentary to cover reggae music in the UK, focusing on a concert at Wembley Stadium in 70. Produced (and funded) by Bamboo Records, directed by Horace Ové and featuring The Pioneers, Desmond Dekker, Millie, The Maytals and DJ Mike Raven. (71)

Woodstock

The Concert for Bangladesh

IMAGINE

Barely released semi-surreal documentary about a day in the life of John Lennon and Yoko Ono, that was co-directed by Lennon and contains music from his LP *'Imagine'* and Yoko Ono's *'Fly'*. Also seen are George Harrison, Andy Warhol, Miles Davis and Phil Spector. (72)

RAGA

Rarely seen Apple Films documentary on the music of Ravi Shankar. (71)

THE LION AT WORLD'S END

Documentary follow up to *Born Free* – this has a plot about a pet lion being relocated from Swinging London to Africa. Soundtrack by Pentangle. (71)

OCEANS

Documentary about surfing, filmed in South Africa, that includes music by The Who and The Moody Blues. (71)

THE CONCERT FOR BANGLADESH

Apple Films feature-length documentary covering the August 71 concert to raise funds for the victims of the cyclone and floods in Bangladesh. Contains footage of George Harrison, Ringo Starr, Klaus Voormann, Ravi Shankar, Eric Clapton and Badfinger. (March 72)

COCKSUCKER BLUES

Feature-length documentary about The Rolling Stones and their 72 tour of the US. Directed by Robert Frank, who made the classic 59 short *Pull My Daisy* with Kerouac, Ginsberg et al. Rarely seen due to the explicit nature of the material it records. (72)

SOUND OF THE CITY: LONDON 1964-1973

Mainly consisting of archive footage, this has The Rolling Stones, Eric Burdon and the Animals, The Crazy World of Arthur Brown, Otis Redding, Pete Townshend, Cream, Steve Winwood, Blind Faith, Cat Stevens, The Jimi Hendrix Experience, Donovan, Joe Cocker, Tina Turner, Pink Floyd and Rod Stewart and The Faces. Directed by Peter Clifton. (73)

GUITARE AU POING

French concert film about the 70 Aix- en-Provence Festival which includes Pete Brown and Piblokto!, Colosseum, Majority One, Rare Bird, Mungo Jerry, Trader Horne, Radha Krishna Temple and Wallace Collection. (June 73)

THE LONDON ROCK AND ROLL SHOW

Peter Clifton documentary covering the August 72 concert at Wembley Stadium. Most of the acts are 50s stars but Wizzard and MC5 also appear, as do Dr Feelgood (backing Heinz). Mick Jagger is interviewed. Directed by Peter Clifton with Peter Whitehead as one of the cameramen and produced by the same company that made *The Punk Rock Movie* in 78. (December 73)

IL DIO SOTTO LA PELLE
(GOD UNDER THE SKIN)

Italian documentary featuring two songs by Catherine Howe. (74)

APPENDIX 3

Shorts

PINK FLOYD LONDON '66-'67

Peter Whitehead film record of Pink Floyd playing at the legendary 14 Hour Technicolour Dream concert in May 67. Glimpsed are John Lennon and Yoko Ono, not at that point an item. (67)

THE IMAGE

Michael Armstrong-directed horror short starring David Bowie. Armstrong later scripted *The Haunted House of Horror.* (67)

THE TORTOISE AND THE HARE

Made by Hugh Hudson and David Cammell with music by the Spencer Davis Group. (67)

THE LONE RANGER

Short film made by Pete Townshend (and possibly Speedy Keen) and also – briefly – mooted as the title of a future Who LP. (68)

IMPROVISATION SUR UN DIMANCHE APRES-MIDI

Rarely seen Salvador Dali short that includes UK pop-psych outfit Nirvana. (68)

DOLLY STORY

Robert Amram-directed film with Chris Farlowe and Swinging London hairdresser Vidal Sassoon. (68)

BEYOND IMAGE

BFI short featuring the music of Soft Machine. (69)

DEATH MAY BE YOUR SANTA CLAUS

Made by Frankie Dymon Jr.– a follower of Michael X – who can also be seen in a small acting role in Godard's *Sympathy for the Devil.* Fantasy about a radical black student who dreams of having a white girlfriend. Filmed in derelict areas near Notting Hill and Ladbroke Grove, with a soundtrack by Second Hand. (69)

Pink Floyd London 66-67

Invocation of My Demon Brother

INVOCATION OF MY DEMON BROTHER

Kenneth Anger film, with a soundtrack of synthesiser music played by Mick Jagger. The Rolling Stones appear, as do Anita Pallenberg and Anton LaVey, leader of US cult the Church of Satan. (69)

TWENTY NINE

Alexis Kanner stars in drama about a man waking up in a strange house after a night out. Music by Tuesday's Children. Went out as the supporting film to *If…* (January 69)

LES BICYCLETTES DE BELSIZE

Twenty nine minute cinema drama, directed by Douglas Hickox who went on from this to *Entertaining Mr Sloane*. Soundtrack was by Les Reed and Barry Mason and includes a song by Episode Six. Title theme was a big hit for Engelbert Humperdinck. (69)

A STONE IN THE BUSH

Australian short about the filming of Ned Kelly. Mick Jagger appears and there is some music from The Rolling Stones. (March 70)

GRAVE NEW WORLD

Early example of a promotional film. Made to showcase The Strawbs and their LP of the same name. (February 72)

PLOD

Adaptation of a Roger McGough book, with The Scaffold. (72)

LUCIFER RISING

Kenneth Anger fantasy, heavily influenced by Aleister Crowley, that includes Marianne Faithfull, Jimmy Page, Chris Jagger and Donald Cammell Partly filmed at Avebury stone circle in Wiltshire. (72)

MALTAMOUR

Documentary about Malta that has a soundtrack by Pete Brown and Graham Bond. (73)

APPENDIX 4

TV Musical Specials, Documentaries, Concerts

LUCY IN LONDON

Lucille Ball visits London, is escorted (in a motor bike and sidecar) around the sites by Anthony Newley and meets, among others, The Dave Clark Five and Peter Wyngarde. Music and title song were by Phil Spector. (October 66)

VIBRATO

Belgian TV special, featuring The Rolling Stones. (January 67)

SWINGING LONDON

Belgian TV concert film, with Helen Shapiro, The Kinks and Engelbert Humperdinck. (March 67)

THE RECORD STAR SHOW

BBC coverage of Wembley concert with Alan Price, Paul Jones, Lulu, The Tremeloes, The New Vaudeville Band and Geno Washington and The Ram Jam Band. (April 67)

THE RAVERS

Episode of BBC TV series *Man Alive* that covers the emerging 'groupie' phenomenon and features Simon Dupree and the Big Sound. (June 67)

LE PARAPLUIE DES VEDETTES

French pop musical with Johnny Hallyday and Françoise Hardy. UK actress/singer Carol Friday also appears. (August 67)

THE CAT STEVENS SHOW

Belgian TV special, hosted by Cat Stevens and featuring Whistling Jack Smith, Paul and Barry Ryan, The Mindbenders, Jackie Trent, Double Feature, The New Inspiration and Friday Brown. (November 67)

VIBRATO

Belgian TV special, featuring Pink Floyd, Oscar (Paul Nicholas), PP Arnold and Serge Gainsbourg. (February 68)

BROTHERS NO MORE

ITV documentary about The Walker Brothers farewell tour of Japan. (March 68)

FRANKIE HOWERD MEETS THE BEE GEES

Thames TV special, scripted by Galton and Simpson, that includes The Bee Gees and

Julie Driscoll and Brian Auger and The Trinity. (August 68)

A YEAR IN THE LIFE

BBC documentary about The Mike Stuart Span and their difficulties in 68. (68)

JOLIE POUPÉE

French TV special that includes Joe Cocker. (December 68)

THE LIVERPOOL SCENE

Granada TV series, built around the poetry, music and general observations of the Liverpool Scene. (February 69)

UNTERWEGS NACH KATHMANDU

West German TV film that includes music from King Crimson and Ravi Shankar. (November 71)

SYMPATHY FOR THE DEVIL

West German TV series that includes music from Maggie Bell (January 1972)

APPENDIX 5

TV Dramas

NIGHT CLUB

Belgian TV comedy, featuring Dave Berry.
(October 66)

THE FANTASIST

Episode of BBC *Theatre 625* drama series,
written by Alun Owen and starring James Villiers
and Charlotte Rampling. Gordon Waller appears
in a supporting role and Marmalade feature in a
music sequence. (May 67)

THE FURTHER ADVENTURES
OF LUCKY JIM

BBC TV series, written by Dick Clement and
Ian La Frenais, that updates the Kingsley Amis
character from the 50s to the 60s. Title music by
Alan Price. (May 67)

BOY MEETS GIRL

BBC TV series that ran from 67-69. The title
theme, by Ron Grainer, was later rocked up and
released as a single by Paper Blitz Tissue.
(August 67)

DEATH OF A PRIVATE

BBC TV Wednesday Play. Paper Blitz Tissue
appear as The Majors. Music by Ron Grainer.
Charles Stuart also appears as a pop singer: he
released a single on RCA at this time.
(December 67)

THE PISTOL SHOT

BBC *Theatre 625* adaptation of Pushkin story that
has an acting role for David Bowie, billed fourth
in the cast. (May 68)

THE QUEEN STREET GANG

Thames TV series about the adventures of a
group of children. Music by Arzachel. (August 68)

WHERE WAS SPRING?

BBC TV comedy series, with Eleanor Bron and
John Bird. Artwork by Klaus Voormann and
music by The Kinks. (January 69)

RAPE

Austrian TV film, made by John Lennon and Yoko
Ono. (March 69)

TAKE THREE GIRLS

BBC TV series about the tribulations of three
young women sharing a flat in London in the late
60s. Theme song by Pentangle. (69)

ROUND FOUR

Episode of Granada TV series *The Contenders*
(based on the John Wain novel) that includes
Wayne Fontana in an acting role and an
appearance by The Elastic Band. (September 69)

THE SEASON OF THE WITCH

BBC TV production – as part of *The Wednesday Play* series – that stars Julie Driscoll and Paul Nicholas. (January 70)

RUMOUR

One of the ITV *Playhouse* series that was written and directed by Mike Hodges, immediately before he started *Get Carter*. Soundtrack by The Moody Blues. (March 70)

NO TRAMS TO LIME STREET

Remake of the Alun Owen play (also broadcast in 59) shown as part of the BBC *Wednesday Play* series. Music by Marty Wilde. (March 70)

THE LONG DISTANCE PIANO PLAYER

Broadcast as the first of the BBC TV *Play for Today* series. Stars Ray Davies. (October 70)

LONG VOYAGE OUT OF WAR

BBC TV mini-series about a group of characters during and after the Second World War. Original music by Alan Price. (71)

MAN FRIDAY

One of the BBC TV *Play for Today* series, stars Ram John Holder as Man Friday and has music by Mike Westbrook. (October 72)

HOME

Lindsay Anderson directed version of the David Storey play, broadcast as part of the BBC TV *Play for Today* series. Original music by Alan Price. Not the first TV adaptation of this: a similar production, with the same principals, appeared in the US on *Net Playhouse* in February 68. (January 72)

HAIR TRIGGER

Part of the BBC TV *Doomwatch* series, about a secret government department that battles against environmental and technological disasters. Features music by The Fortunes. (July 72)

THE PROTECTORS

A Gerry Anderson drama series, made for ITV, about a privately-funded secret international crime fighting syndicate, starring Robert Vaughn, late of *The Man From U.N.C.L.E.*, and set partly in London. Theme song (*'Avenues and Alleyways'*) performed by Tony Christie. (September 72)

WHATEVER HAPPENED TO THE LIKELY LADS?

BBC comedy series with James Bolam and Rodney Bewes (previously seen in *The Likely Lads*, 64-66 and key supporting actors in many UK 'kitchen sink' dramas of the early 60s). Set on Tyneside with a theme song by Mike Hugg and Tony Rivers. (January 73)

AFTERWORD

This book began life as a series of articles that appeared in *Lobster*, about the late Simon Dee and UK Pirate Radio in the 60s and 70s, and in *Shindig*, on the career of pop entrepreneur Ronan O'Rahilly and the back story to the Paul Jones/Pink Floyd film *The Committee*. Whilst writing these, and researching the book project that gradually emerged, I spoke to Phillip Goodhand-Tait about *Universal Soldier*; Les Reed about *The Girl On A Motorcycle* and much else; Bob Levis about *Gold*; Peter Prentice on the now virtually impossible to see *Popdown*; Max Steuer about *The Committee* and his experience of working with Pink Floyd (and Syd Barrett); Mike Plumley, a friend and confidante of Ronan O'Rahilly; Revel Guest about *London Rock*; Mike d'Abo on *There's a Girl in My Soup*; John Tebb (one time keyboards player and vocalist in The Casuals) about *Seven Times Seven*; Andy 'Thunderclap' Newman about *Not Tonight, Darling* and the Shulman brothers about their time in Simon Dupree and the Big Sound and, subsequently, Gentle Giant, life on the road and their involvement in various TV productions. I am grateful for the time they gave and the memories they shared.

Thanks are due to Robin Ramsay, publisher of *Lobster*, who published my early pieces on Dee and Pirate Radio; to my brother Sean, who spent many hours of his time copying and reproducing images and assembling the work into a format that would appeal to a publisher; and to Sean MacBride, an old friend and one time musical colleague who suggested helpful alterations and embellishments to the foreword.

Inevitably, much of the research required for a project of this type was carried out by scouring the internet – a medium that continues to expand and provide further information. The parameters within which the research was carried out were set as specifically as possible beforehand: any film with a UK pop group or pop singer acting, performing in a scene (or scenes), credited with the title song/theme or making a contribution to the soundtrack. UK productions that met this were included, as were a number of European films, but US films set wholly in the US were not... after all, these could hardly be considered to be part of Swinging London. In the last resort, judgements had to be made, and whenever they were, the logic of candidates for inclusion meeting the UK film-UK pop music axis was paramount: hence the absence of *Barbarella*, *Arabesque*, *The Italian Job*, *Get Carter* and many others from the main narrative. Within this context, every attempt has been made to assemble a comprehensive listing. And to check, as far as practicable, the material posted on the internet, not all of which is one hundred per cent accurate. For instance: some of the film posters for *Alba pagana/May Morning* claim Iain Sinclair as a co-star. Is this the same Iain Sinclair, colleague of JG Ballard and Michael Moorcock, who currently publishes psycho-geographical works? It might have been... as he also dabbled in some minor film work and acting during the period. Enquiries to the man himself soon scotched the idea – it wasn't him at all but an Ian Sinclair (the posters were misspelt), a now forgotten minor actor of the period.

The internet clearly has its surprises. Not everything is online, even now, and it was useful to have access to dusty old film magazines and books from thirty to forty years ago, including *The NME Guide to Rock Cinema* (80) and *Twenty Years of Movie Rock* (74), the latter mentioning a number of productions about which further information is still lacking forty years later. It is entirely possible that a battered and previously forgotten soundtrack LP will turn up in a car boot sale or charity shop, featuring a UK group performing in a film that died at the box office in the 60s (or wasn't even released – anyone for *The Other People?*); never made it to video in the 70s and 80s; or, even if it did, typically sold only a few copies in non-UK domains before being deleted. Within a few days of any artefact like this being discovered, the contents will be posted on YouTube and a number of blogs will promote them enthusiastically. A CD reissue will follow, as will a DVD with 'extras'. A year on, and the item will be an essential component and reference for students of the period and lovers of this now distant era in British artistic achievement.

There is always the possibility of being pleasantly surprised.

Simon Matthews

INDEX

Emerson, Lake and Palmer, 183, 195

Emery, Dick, 71, 113

Emmanuelle, 77

Emotions, 87

Emperor Rosko, 172

End, The, 42

Endfield, Cy, 146

English Rose, 115

Entertaining Mr Sloane, 15, 113, 120, 140, 181, 200

Episode Six, 44, 200

Epstein, Brian, 113

Equipe 84, 96

Essex, David, 47, 151, 175, 185, 193, 195

Evans, Barry, 54

Evans, Mal, 188

Evening of British Rubbish, An (stage review), 75

Every Day's a Holiday, 101

Every Home Should Have One, 192

Every Mother's Son, 106

Experience, 137, 197

Expresso Bongo, 18

Exton, Clive, 120

Extremes, 145

Eyes of Blue, The, 109

Eyewitness, 117, 171

F

Fabricius, Bent, 69

Faces, The, 170, 197, 198

Factor, Donald, 146

Fairfield Parlour, 117

Fairport Convention, 164, 197

Faith, Adam, 44, 185

Faithfull, Marianne, 38, 77, 80, 94, 102, 112, 135, 144, 189, 191, 196, 200

Fame, Georgie, 52, 59, 120, 140, 163, 168, 181

Family, 94, 156, 164

Family Life, 132

Family Way, The, 37, 54, 68, 110

Fantasist, The (TV), 202

Fantoni, Barry, 39

Far from the Madding Crowd, 17

Farewell Concert, 197

Faris, Alexander, 29

Farlowe, Chris, 53, 199

Farmer, Mimsy, 92

Farr, Gary, 57

Farrow, Mia, 126, 127

Fassbinder, Rainer Werner, 16, 32, 138, 149

Fast Kill, The, 160

Fata Morgana, 159, 184

Fathom, 55

Feast, Michael, 152

Feldman, Marty, 192

Feldmarescialla, La, 30

Fellini, Federico, 35, 118, 124, 190

Female Eunuch, The, 146

Ferris Wheel, 81

Ferzetti, Gabriele, 76, 111

Fiddy, John, 142

Fields, Duggie, 21

File of the Golden Goose, The, 180

Final Programme, The, 128, 177, 182

Finch, Jon, 155, 177, 178

Findlay, Jack, 162

Finlay, Frank, 46

Finney, Albert, 40, 59, 62, 187, 194

First Step on the Moon, The (song), 58

Fisher, Matthew, 59

Fist of Fury, 21

Five's Company, 36

Flanagan, 115

Fleming, Ian, 27, 105, 107, 112

Flirtations, The, 45

Flower Pot Men, The, 49

Fly (LP), 198

Flying Burrito Brothers, The, 133

Fonda, Jane, 28

Fool, The, 15, 68

Fool in Love, A, 144

For the Love of Ada, 195

For Those Who Think Young, 93

Ford, Derek, 115, 119

Forever More, 160

Forman, Milos, 193

Formula V, 31

Forster-Jones, Glenna, 124

Fortunes, The, 44, 145, 203

Foss, Chris, 183

Foster, Julia, 25, 26

Foundations, The, 103, 122, 139

Four Dimensions of Greta, 163

Four in the Morning, 59

Foursome/Sweet and Sexy, 144

Fox, Edward, 46

Fox, James, 126, 127, 128

Foy, Eddie Jr, 62

Frame, Pete, 87

Frampton, Peter, 186

Frances, Stephen, 102

Francis, Clive, 120, 140

Francis, Freddie, 186

Franco, Jesus, 93, 154

Frank, Robert, 198

Frankie Howerd Meets the Bee Gees, 113, 201

Frankovich, MJ, 136

Freedom, The, 64, 65, 181

Freedom to Love, 155

Freeman, Gillian, 77

Freeman, Robert, 81, 82

Frestonia, 124

Friday, Carol, 201

Friends, 141

Frisby, Terence, 136

Froese, Edgar, 156

Frog, Wynder K, 81, 173

Frugal Sound, The, 30

Fuest, Robert, 39, 177

Funeral in Berlin, 67

Further Adventures of Lucky Jim, The (TV), 187

Fury, Billy, 46, 176

G

Gainsbourg, Serge, 13, 18, 38, 83, 102, 111, 112, 121, 161, 201

Galactic Federation, The, 58

Galton, Ray, 113, 201

Game, The, 101

Game is Over, The (Curée, La), 28, 38, 120

Gardner, Ava, 134

Garnett, Tony, 131, 132

R

Raben, Peer, 149
Radha Krishna Temple, 198
Radio Caroline, 22, 77, 125, 146, 148, 166
Radio Luxembourg, 127
Radio North Sea International, 45
Radio One, 90, 117, 154
Raga, 198
Ragazza Nuda/Strip-Tease, Una, 13
Raggazi di Bandiera Gialla I, 96
Raging Moon, The, 192
Ragovoy, Jerry, 101
Rags, JP, 88, 181
Ram-Jam (TV), 30
Rampling, Charlotte, 29, 112, 182, 183, 202
Randall and Hopkirk (Deceased) (TV), 118
Rape (TV), 202
Rare Bird, 198
Rattles, The, 30
Raven, Mike, 90, 154, 197
Ravers, The (TV), 201
Ready Steady Go! (TV), 20, 80
Rebel, The, 113
Reckoning, 15, 89
Record Star Show, The, 201
Red Sun (Rote Sonne), 192
Redding, Otis, 197, 198
Redgrave, Lynn, 29, 47, 84
Redgrave, Michael, 109, 118
Redgrave, Vanessa, 36, 131
Reed, Les, 43, 44, 77, 87, 200, 205
Reed, Oliver, 12, 17, 26, 46, 59, 103
Reflections on Love, 68
Reggae, 197
Reid, Beryl, 120, 122
Reid, Terry, 130, 164
Remick, Lee, 113
Remo Four, The, 68, 181
Renaissance, 176
Renbourn, John, 159
Renegade Gun, 96
Renegades, The, 30, 96, 190

residencia, La (House that Screamed, The), 31
Revolution, 161
Richards, Keith, 176, 195
Richmond, Fiona, 144
Riley, Bridget, 27
Riot on Sunset Strip, 92
Rise and Rise of Michael Rimmer, The, 119
River Deep, Mountain High, 128
Rivers, Tony, 203
Robbery, 161
Roberts, Christian, 51
Robinson, Bruce, 152
Robson, Flora, 122
Rock Dreams (book), 43, 48
Rockford Files, The (TV), 45
Rocky Horror Show, The, 140, 151
Roeg, Nicolas, 126, 127, 128, 164
Rogers, Julie, 189
Rogers, Tristan, 163
Rohm, Maria, 93
Rohmer, Eric, 41
Rokes, The, 96
Roller Girl, 38
Rolling Stones, The, 17, 20, 33, 34, 42
Rolling Stones Rock and Roll Circus, The, 80, 90, 128
Rollins, Sonny, 26
Romeo and Juliet, 99, 141
Romero, George A., 195
Room at the Bottom, 101
Rosa Bosom (robot), 75
Rose, Jeremy, 171
Ross, Annie, 154
Rossington, Norman, 13, 171
Round Table, The, 182
Roundhouse, The, 94, 104, 106
Rowan and Martin's Laugh-In, 99, 136
Rowles, John, 107
Roy Young Band, The, 194
Royal Court Theatre, The, 22, 62, 167
Royal Hunt of the Sun, The, 84
Royal Shakespeare Company, The, 70
Rumour, 203

Run with the Wind, 160
Runacre, Jenny, 178
Running Jumping and Standing Still Film, The, 13
Running Scared, 66
Russell, Ken, 18
Russell, Leon, 66, 186
Rustichelli, Carlo, 76
Ryan, Patrick, 50
Ryan, Paul and Barry, 44, 55, 201

S

Sainte-Marie, Buffy, 128
Salad Days (song), 59
Salisbury (LP), 142
Salome, 20, 21, 192
Salt and Pepper, 114
Sam Apple Pie, 116, 164
San Domingo, 32
San Francisco, 21
Sanders, George, 173, 186
Sanders, Pharoah, 116
Sandford, Chris, 125
Sandford, Jeremy, 63
Sapho ou la fureur d'aimer (Sex is my Game), 32
Sarne, Mike, 82, 83, 189
Sarno, Joseph, 129
Sassoon, Vidal, 199
Saturday Night and Sunday Morning, 13, 48, 62, 69, 186, 187
Saturday Night Fever, 135
Saturday Night Out, 115
Satyricon, 118
Saucer Full of Secrets, A (LP), 169
Saxon, Peter, 102
Scaffold, The, 104, 170, 192, 195, 200
Schell, Catherine, 95
Schifano, Mario, 195
Schlesinger, John, 193
Schlöndorff, Volker, 42
Schneider, Romy, 78, 170
Schroeder, Barbet, 41, 92, 165
Schygulla, Hanna, 149
Scofield, Paul, 161
Scorsese, Martin, 127